HOME-BASED BUSINESS SERIES

How to Start a Home-Based
Craft Business

Fourth Edition

Kenn Oberrecht

The
Globe
Pequot
Press

GUILFORD, CONNECTICUT

Cover design by Nancy Freeborn
Text design by Mary Ballachino
Cover photos: Painted eggs by Peter Ardito, Index Stock; pottery ©2003 www.clipart.com

ISSN 1546-671X
ISBN 0-7627-2833-7

Manufactured in the United States of America
Fourth Edition/First Printing

For my good friend Peggy Patton

Contents

Introduction

Have we met? I feel as if I know you. Let me see if I have it right. You're a creative person, and you like working with your hands. You enjoy crafts as a hobby and have gotten pretty good at what you do. Many of your friends and relatives proudly display the craft items you have given them at Christmas, for birthdays, and on other gift-giving occasions.

You've probably won some ribbons at the county fair or at some local craft-club exhibits. You've gained confidence in yourself and in your craft. People have told you time and again that you should be selling what you make, and you've begun to believe them. After all, you've seen far worse on sale at gift shops, galleries, and craft fairs. You wonder how a person might go about getting into the business. The idea's a little scary, but it's exciting too.

Wouldn't it be great to chuck the nine-to-five, be your own boss, and run your own business your way? No more long, boring, and costly commutes. No more workplace hassles and politics. You'll start pocketing the profits instead of making profits for others. And take a day off now and then simply because you want to. It's possible, isn't it?

Of course it's possible. It's even probable, if you put your mind to it, research the prospects, develop a sound plan, and stay on course. What's more, it won't cost as much as you might think.

You no doubt already own some of the necessary equipment and can afford to buy the required materials. You possess important knowledge and experience in at least one craft, or you're willing to learn. Best of all, as a home-based entrepreneur, you won't have to borrow a bundle to pay the lease on a shop downtown or at the mall.

In most ways, starting and running your own home-based craft business is probably easier than you think; in a few ways, it might be a little tougher, but there are no obstacles impossible to surmount. In the pages that follow, you'll find a wealth of valuable business information and many helpful tips and tricks that will take the edge off that little pang of fear and give you the courage to take the big step.

So this is a book for artisans, but it's not about any specific craft. Rather, it covers the craft *business* and tells you what you need to know about operating such a business from your home. In the following chapters, you'll find practical solutions to problems and plenty of solid advice on how to tap your creative skills to earn a living.

If you haven't inherited millions or won the lottery, you're going to have to work for a living for the rest of your life. Why not make a career of doing what you most enjoy? It won't just happen, but you can make it happen.

Chapter One

Starting Your Home-Based Craft Business

Among the many businesses that can be operated from a home, craft businesses are particularly suitable. Most craft objects are relatively small and easy to store and transport. The tools are easy to use at home and won't disturb your neighbors. Manufacturing materials aren't gravely hazardous and probably won't pose any major storage problems.

Craft professionals shouldn't find working at home any more difficult than craft hobbyists do. Depending on your craft, the transition from hobbyist to professional requires little or no adjustment in the way you manufacture your products. You may already have sufficient work space in the form of a shop or workroom. Because you will be increasing production volume, you will probably have to find or create adequate storage space, and you'll want an office of some sort for attending to all the details of running a business.

For many would-be artisan-entrepreneurs, it's difficult to muster the necessary confidence to approach the marketplace. Confidence is every bit as important as skill in your chosen craft. You must have confidence in your craft, in yourself, and in your ability to run a business and sell your products.

Don't think of your products as homemade, but rather as meticulously handcrafted to exacting standards. Handcrafted products are in great demand, because they provide customers with an elusive quality too infrequently encountered these days: good old Yankee craftsmanship. Carefully handcrafted products are better made than assembly-line stampouts and are unique because of their quality.

Look Before You Leap

Before getting down to the business of business, you have some pleasant preliminary work ahead of you. Visit the kinds of shops, galleries, and stores in which you would like to see your products sold. Browse, observe the customers, talk to the proprietors, and ask for advice.

Attend local and nearby arts-and-crafts shows, Christmas bazaars, sidewalk exhibits, wine festivals, food fairs, and other events where there are craft booths and displays. Look for ideas and take notes. Watch the customers to see what stops them and what entices them to buy. Talk to the exhibitors when they're not busy. Ask them about their experiences and tell them of your plans. Seek the advice of these readily available experts.

Don't trust your memory. Take notes, and later review them carefully. You'll be surprised how the ideas you find will breed others. Jot them down too. All this will become a solid foundation upon which to build a secure business.

Should You Start Your Own Business?

No one but you can determine whether or not you should start your own craft business, but certain indicators can lead you toward the right choice. Of course, if you have little or no skill in any craft, minimal manual dexterity, and no interest in getting better, you needn't go any further; find yourself another business. If, on the other hand, you're a competent artisan—even a good one—but have no patience for or interest in managing a business, then you'd better work for someone else for the rest of your career and treat crafts as a hobby.

Even if the notion of being self-employed as a home-based artisan appeals to you, and you either now possess or are willing to attain the necessary skills and knowledge, you still must question yourself thoroughly to learn where your strengths and weaknesses lie. This is part of the planning stage of your business: a process that's never too early to start and one that should continue throughout the life of your business.

Market Survey—Retail Outlet

Business _____   Contact Date _____

Street _____   Contact _____

Suite _____ P.O. Box _____   Title _____

City _____   Phone (___) _____

State _____ Zip _____   Phone (___) _____

Weekday Hours _____   Fax (___) _____

Saturday Hours _____   E-mail _____

Sunday Hours _____   Days Closed _____

____ Gallery   ____ Gift Shop   ____ Department Store

____ General Store   ____ Craft Shop   ____ Craft Mall

____ Antiques Shop   ____ Antiques Mall   ____ Toy Store

____ Other _____

Description of Merchandise _____

_____

_____

Best-Selling Items _____

_____

Visit/Interview Notes & Comments _____

_____

_____

_____

_____

Market Survey—Retail Outlet

Business _The Country Mercantile_   Contact Date _February 18, 2003_

Street _1615 River Road_   Contact _Lily Putian_

Suite _____ P.O. Box _1851_   Title _Owner_

City _Connorsville_   Phone (800) _555-5432_

State _Indiana_   Zip _47331_   Phone (123) _555-9876_

Weekday Hours _10:00 am to 6:00 pm_   Fax (123) _555-9898_

Saturday Hours _9:00 am to 6:00 pm_   E-mail _LilyPut@Indiana.store.net_

Sunday Hours _Noon to 5:00 pm_   Days Closed _Monday_

____ Gallery   ____ Gift Shop   ____ Department Store

_X_ General Store   ____ Craft Shop   ____ Craft Mall

____ Antiques Shop   ____ Antiques Mall   ____ Toy Store

____ Other _____

Description of Merchandise _Clothing, boots, specialty and gourmet foods,_

cookware, cutlery, kitchen utensils, small appliances, canning

equipment and supplies, mugs, glasses, wine, microbrews, books.

Best-Selling Items _Anything for the kitchen and cooking._

_____

Visit/Interview Notes & Comments _Lily is interested in carrying alder mug_

trees, laminated cutlery blocks, hardwood herb & spice jars, and

maple cutting boards. Will be buying stock in April; I should phone

or send order sheet. She wants ONE GIANT MUG TREE IMMEDIATELY.

Agreed to deliver by March 15.

Below are ten questions you need to answer in as much detail as possible before you start your business. So sit down with a pen and a pad of paper, and answer as many of them as you can. You probably won't be able to respond to all the questions in one sitting. Those left unanswered will guide you toward your weaknesses or the areas where you simply need to do some work or research, or perhaps seek help.

Answer the questions as completely and honestly as possible; to do less is to fool yourself and court disaster.

1. *Why do you want to start a home-based craft business?* Provide as many reasons as you can, such as being your own boss, having an opportunity to spend more time with your family, gaining control of your career, getting out of a dead-end job, avoiding the hassles of commuting, and anything else you can think of.

2. *What craft experience and management skills can you bring to your new business?* List craft-related jobs and management positions you've held, courses you've taken, books you've read, and how they have helped to prepare you. If you identify weaknesses in either area, explain how you plan to overcome them. If you've never held a management position, perhaps your plan to gain the necessary skills is to launch a research effort at your local library and bookstore, to take business courses at a local community college, to sign up for seminars offered by a small-business organization or cooperative, or a combination of these.

3. *How much space will you need for your new business?* First, determine what kind of space you will need: office, workshop, studio, warehouse or storage room, sales area or display room. Every home-based business must have an office. You'll need some kind of workroom, workshop, studio, or a combination of these. Nobody ever has enough storage space. Although some businesses might get by with no more than a large storage cabinet or closet, most craft businesses require more, some far more. After determining your space requirements, estimate the size in square feet. Sit down with paper, pencil, and ruler and lay out your work area. (If you own a computer, there are programs that will help you do this.) Allow for furniture and equipment so that you'll get an idea of how much space this business is going to take up. (For more information, see Chapter 2 under "Setting Up Your Business Space.")

4. *How do you plan to accommodate the space demands of your new business?* Will you temporarily set up a home office at one end of the dining-room table or put a desk in your bedroom and work there? There is nothing wrong with that; many home-based entrepreneurs start out this way. Will you set up a permanent office in an unused room? Can your office double as a studio or workroom, or do you need separate rooms? Do you have garage, basement, or attic space you can convert? Can you build on? Everyone will have different answers to these questions; renters are more restricted than owners, and persons who live in small dwellings are more restricted than those who have plenty of space. For some, the answers might change within a short time. If you plan to move within the next five years, you would do well to list short-term and long-term space considerations. (Chapter 7, "Taxes and Record Keeping," covers the use of a home as a business.)

5. *What are your immediate and future equipment needs and how will you meet them?* List all arts-and-crafts equipment you will need to start and operate your business for one year. Depending on the nature of your craft(s), that could include a wide assortment of hand tools, power tools, and various specialized instruments. List all office and other equipment you will need for the same period: computer, telephones, calculator, filing cabinets, office furniture, vehicle. Similarly, list your projected equipment needs for the next five years. In each category, indicate equipment you already own and note how you expect to acquire what you don't have. Keep in mind that in addition to acquiring equipment, you'll probably need to update and upgrade some during your first five years of business. (See Chapter 2 under "Setting Up Your Business Space.")

6. *What licenses, permits, and laws do you need to know about to operate a business from your home?* Laws vary from state to state, county to county, and city to city. Your state may require you to file your business name with a state agency or to apply for a business or vendor's license. You might have to obtain a permit from your county government. There could be city ordinances regulating the operation of home businesses, even from one neighborhood to the next. You need to know about all such obstacles and determine how you'll overcome them before you go into business. (Chapter 5, "The Legal Aspects of Your Craft Business," offers more information on zoning ordinances, licenses, and permits.)

7. *How much cash will you need to run your business for one year and where will it come from?* This is no place to fudge the figures. Be as honest and as accurate as possible, even though you're making an estimate, and possibly not a very educated one at that. Remember, if you must err on money matters, it's always best to err on the side of fiscal conservatism: Overestimate the payables and underestimate the receivables—any outcome to the contrary will be a pleasant surprise. Estimate what it will cost you to run the business for a year, and don't forget to include your own salary as part of the cost. Now determine where the operating capital will come from: savings, spouse's income, pension or retirement income, the business itself, or elsewhere. (For more information on financial planning, see Chapters 3 and 6.)

8. *Who are your competitors, how are they doing, and how do you expect to overtake them in the marketplace?* The way you deal with this question depends on the kinds of craftwork you plan to engage in and how many other local artisans work in the same area. If certain kinds of crafts are popular in your community or region, and you plan to work with those same crafts, you'll be in competition with many other local artisans. If they're all driving fancy vehicles and living in expensive houses, there's obviously plenty of room for competition. If they're barely scratching out an existence, however, that could mean the supply is outstripping the demand, and you might need to look for another niche. Chances are, reality lies somewhere between the two extremes. If you have a particular area of expertise—say, clock making, picture framing, or basket weaving—in a small community, you could be the only artisan so skilled and may well fill a niche. Spend some time with this question, and answer it carefully. This is your first step into the realm of market analysis. (You'll find more marketing information and ideas in Chapter 10, "Marketing Your Craft Business.")

9. *What are your short-term financial and personal goals for your new business?* In other words, what do you expect to earn and accomplish during your first year of operation? This question relates to question 1 and goes beyond question 7. Here you need to focus, get more specific. You should lay out objectives that go beyond mere subsistence or "just getting by." What are your goals? What do you expect your income to be by the end of your first year? Will you have others working for you? What sort of hourly or daily rates or commission fees will you

be demanding by then? How will you have improved or branched out? What will you have learned?

10. *What are your long-term financial and personal goals?* Now discuss everything you covered in question 9 in terms of a five-year plan. How big do you expect your business to be in five years? How skilled an artisan do you hope to be? What sort of customers do you expect to have by then? Will your business continue to grow, or will you want it to level off at some point? Do you plan to hire help? Will you branch out into other crafts, arts, and allied fields? Will you get rich?

Hobby vs. Business

Just as there are amateur athletes who are as skilled as or better than their professional counterparts, many serious amateur artists and artisans are every bit as good as most of the people who make a living in their field. The difference has less to do with proficiency than what people choose to do with it.

The distinction used to be a simple one: Amateurs don't get paid for their work; professionals do. That line has been blurred considerably in recent years. While many amateurs are satisfied to treat crafts as a hobby—creating objects for their own enjoyment and perhaps entering amateur competitions to win ribbons and the occasional plum prize—some sell their work to help defray costs. Whether it's a hobby, an avocation, or a profession, a craft can be expensive. Most materials are costly and the equipment sometimes outrageously so. As a hobbyist, you might be able to offset some of your expenses by selling your work. As a professional, you'd better be able to sell enough to pay all your expenses and make a decent profit as well.

One of the most attractive aspects of craftwork is the possibility of advancing from hobby to career, a sequence practitioners of other professions seldom enjoy. We don't see amateur contractors, for example, building houses and office complexes for the joy of it, or hobby surgeons doing coronary bypasses evenings and weekends in their spare time. Many artisans, however, work first for the fun of it, then study and master enough techniques to advance to the level of serious amateur, and ultimately put that knowledge and experience to work earning money.

Part Time vs. Full Time

The artisan who decides to work as a home-based professional is faced with deciding between part-time and full-time work. I suspect most of us begin working part time and gradually or eventually steer our businesses into full-time operation. Starting part time offers many advantages, and I recommend you seriously consider this route. Here are some of the things you can do when starting out part time:

- Work at home in your spare time while retaining a full-time job and its steady income.
- Run a part-time home-based craft business and work at another part-time job to make ends meet.
- Retain the benefits package your employer offers while establishing your home-based business.
- Gain professional experience that will prove invaluable when you go full time.
- Set up adequate business facilities in your spare time without financial hardship.
- Gradually invest in craft and office equipment and furniture.
- See to numerous details at your leisure, such as a logo, business cards, letterhead, brochures, and a Yellow Pages listing.
- Set up files and establish customer accounts, vendor accounts, and bank accounts.
- Build an excellent credit rating and a solid professional reputation.
- Let your business grow until it's making your projected or required full-time income.
- Build a cash reserve that's big enough to finance your first year's full-time operation.
- Get a feel for the potential of your business and markets before making a major commitment.

You can do all this and more as a part-time home-based artisan and entrepreneur. You might continue working part time indefinitely, until you feel like going into full-time business. Or you can do as I did: continue stowing away cash from the income of your part-time business while gaining valuable experience in other related fields.

I ran my home-based business part time for nearly four years, enjoying the diversity of the various kinds of work I was involved in while gaining a tremendous amount of experience. By the time I was ready to work full time at it, I was making regular sales and earning a fairly steady income. I had established many contacts, set up good working facilities in my home, acquired the equipment I needed, and built good working files and a reference library. I had also established all the necessary accounts with vendors, banks, and oil and credit-card companies.

Four years as a part-time entrepreneur also enabled me to experiment with a great array of equipment and to gradually acquire more and upgrade what I had. I plowed my first year's part-time income back into the business to upgrade existing equipment. The following year I started investing in new equipment and putting aside some profits to build a cash reserve.

By the time I was ready for my home-based business to become a full-time occupation, all of my equipment was new, nearly new, or in excellent condition, which assured me of good service with minimal downtime.

I bought a new IBM typewriter and a few other office items, as well as several new tools and six months' worth of office supplies and materials. I paid for everything from the business cash reserve I had accumulated in four years of part-time work and had enough left to cover my first year's expenses and salary. I can't think of a safer, more comfortable way to start a full-time, home-based business.

Of course, there is a downside to starting and running a part-time home-based business while trying to hold down a full-time job elsewhere. It's difficult to do justice to your business while giving your best efforts to an employer. Your first loyalties must go to that employer, which is often a stretch and a hectic way to live and work. But it's also excellent training and might be the only feasible way to realize your dream.

Learning Your Craft

I assume that most people who plan to start and operate a home-based craft business already possess some craft skills. At the very least, you should have some grasp of the basic tools and techniques of your chosen craft(s) and an abiding interest in learning as much as possible about every aspect of the business.

Taking Courses

My first recommendation is to take courses from good teachers at a local college, technical school, or arts-and-crafts school. I stress: *good teachers.* The same course can be taught by two different teachers, and the two can be as similar as platinum and pig iron.

Your first job is to find a course. Then you need to determine the quality and competence of the teacher. You can't be shy. Phone or visit the teacher and ask for a summary of what the course will cover. Tell the teacher what you need and expect from the course, and ask if this course will fulfill those requirements. Find out what texts are to be used and review them. Talk to the teacher's former students. You should be able to tell within one or two class meetings whether you've found a guru or a bozo. In case of the latter, drop the course, get your money back, lodge a complaint with the school, and look elsewhere for instruction.

Again, don't be afraid to ask questions, and don't think you'll appear stupid for doing so. As someone who has taught a variety of college courses and workshops that range from basic to graduate level, I can tell you that one of a teacher's greatest rewards is being able to work with inquisitive and interested students—people who are there to learn.

Learning by Reading

Another way to learn is by reading, and even small public libraries generally have dozens of craft titles on their shelves. In the small town where I live, the public library has nearly 500 craft books listed in fifty-eight subject areas.

You probably already know about some of the general and specialized crafts magazines, but you would do well to spend time learning what other periodicals are available. You should subscribe to the best magazines in your field and plan to purchase the better how-to guides and reference manuals as a way of building a good business library.

In the absence of a good basic course, locally available, I recommend a series of trips to bookstores, public and college libraries, and magazine stands. Browse through the craft titles until you find books on crafts you're skilled or interested in. They should be clearly written and well illustrated. Make a list of all the relevant titles and begin investigating them. Quickly skim through the books to determine those that are worth borrowing from a library, those you'll want to buy for your own library, and the poorly written and illustrated books that aren't worth your time and money.

Do the same with magazines. At a good public library and at local magazine stands, you'll find periodicals worth reading, some even worth subscribing to. At the library's reference section, check the *Readers' Guide to Periodical Literature* for titles in your interest areas.

As a crafts professional, you'll want to subscribe to *The Crafts Report,* a magazine that bills itself as "the business journal for the crafts industry." This monthly publication runs regular columns and departments, as well as feature articles on topics of interest and importance to craft professionals. It tracks nationwide trends, announces shows and fairs state by state, and puts readers in touch with peers and prospects. (See the "Source Directory" at the back of this book for more details.)

Don't forget business literature. Investigate the business-book sections at local libraries and bookstores, and pay special attention to volumes prepared for home-based business managers. Do likewise in the computer-book sections. Also review the various business and computer magazines that are available.

If you have Internet access, you can browse the virtual bookshelves at giant on-line bookstores, such as amazon.com and barnesandnoble.com. There you can make general subject searches for craft, business, and computer books. You can also search for specific titles, examine their tables of contents, and read chapter excerpts as well as publishers' and readers' reviews.

You can't conclude this initial research project and consider the job done. You'll have to continue reading books and magazines from now on, not only to learn what you don't yet know, but also to keep abreast of the ever-changing technology.

Workshops and Seminars

You should be able to find craft workshops and business seminars in your part of the country. You'll learn about these in national magazines and local newspapers, as well as through direct-mail advertising once your name and address get established on various mailing lists as those of the owner of a home-based craft business.

Other good sources for information about workshops and seminars are your local chamber of commerce, the business department of any nearby college or university, and your community's Small Business Development Center.

The Optional Apprenticeship

Sometimes it's possible to learn from others as an apprentice of sorts. If you can stand the low pay (usually minimum wage) and gofer chores, working as an assistant to an established artisan can be a good way to learn a craft from an expert. Keep in mind, too, that although your paycheck is small, what you learn on the job might otherwise cost you dearly in the form of tuition paid at a school.

Artist vs. Artisan

Are you an artist or an artisan? Or could you possibly be both? Often, a thin line separates the two categories; sometimes the line is invisible. That is, some artists are also skilled artisans, and a good many artisans are truly artistic in their endeavors. It's often difficult to distinguish artworks from craftworks.

For example, the watercolorist who learns how to mount, mat, and frame watercolors is an artist who engages in a craft to benefit the artwork. A good many artisans clearly have artistic abilities that enhance their craftworks and increase their value and salability.

Some people seem to have innate artistic abilities, but they are the exceptions. Most practicing artists have an aptitude for art but were not born with the skills they possess; they learned them. The same is true of artisans.

Both artists and artisans work with spatial relationships and must be conscious of size, shape, form, design, and composition in their respective works. Therefore, most artisans can profit from the study of art and design. Both fine and applied arts are disciplines you might consider studying as a way of improving your craft and making yourself a more versatile and skilled artisan.

Specialist vs. Generalist

The decision to work as a specialist or generalist depends largely on acquired skills, personal choice, and the realities of the marketplace. Most artisans begin as specialists because their skills are limited. Those who decide to remain specialists usually do so because they enjoy working in one craft area and have found an eager market for their products.

There's certainly nothing wrong with the single-craft approach to the business, as long as you are happy with what you are doing and are generating the kind of income you need or want. Diversifying, however, is a good way to spread out your liabilities, reduce risks, and add other skills to your repertoire. For the person who is easily bored, diversity might be the only route to success in the home-based craft business.

Whether to specialize or generalize is mainly up to you. The only advice I will offer in this regard is to learn your craft well, then evaluate your circumstances in light of the marketplace. If you then wish to begin diversifying, learn your next crafts equally well, one at a time.

You will also probably do best to work in related or similar areas. This will enable you to use some of the tools and equipment required for one craft in other crafts. For example, if you're a woodworker, you'll probably find it relatively easy and inexpensive to move into picture framing or marquetry. The tools and materials you use for making wooden furnishings and fixtures will prove valuable if you start making wooden toys, puzzles, games, models, and decoys. Country, regional, and holiday crafts are other possibilities for the skilled woodworker.

Salable Crafts

For the most part, the home-based artisan can work in any craft area. Your options are manifold. You can pick the craft you're best at or most interested in and build a business around that. You can specialize or diversify. To compete as a specialist—say, in ceramics—you should set out to become the best ceramist in your community. If you decide to work in several or many handicrafts, you needn't strive to be, and probably won't be, the best in your community in each craft. You'll have to be good in each, though, and should strive to be outstanding. You might thereby prove yourself the most versatile artisan in your vicinity.

Popular American Crafts

Calligraphy	Stained glass projects	Tole painting
Toy making	Making puzzles	Making games
Jewelry making	Cloisonné enameling	Leather craft
Ceramics	Pottery	Needlecraft
Making decoys	Building clocks	Kitchen crafts
Basketry	Picture framing	Textile crafts
Candle making	Tile craft	Block printing
Silk-screening	Beadwork	Decoupage
Plastics & acrylics	Doll making	Rug making
Macramé	Knife making	Making fishing tackle
Gunsmithing	Folk art	Making archery tackle
Silversmithing	Coppersmithing	Blacksmithing
Tincrafting	Woodworking	Marquetry
Wood carving	Sign making	Country crafts
Regional crafts	Native crafts	Holiday crafts
Garden crafts	Yard crafts	Nautical crafts
Model making		Glassblowing

It's important that you have some idea of the direction you want your business to take, and, again, planning is crucial. You guessed it: It's time, once more, for the trusty pad and pen. List all the crafts you can think of. Identify those that interest you most. If you can, pick the one that's most exciting to you; if you can't, don't worry about it.

I was able to come up with a list of fifty popular American crafts, which I'm including here as a way of helping you create your own list. See if you can add to it. Then highlight those that appeal most to you.

By performing this simple exercise, you may have already identified the craft you are most suited for and might want to specialize in. On the other hand, you may have discovered that your interests are broad and that you are most inclined to be a diversified artisan.

You needn't set out immediately to specialize in anything, or to generalize, for that matter. You could find in a year or two that you're being pulled one way or another. It doesn't matter. As long as you continue to stay in touch with your own feelings and ambitions, as long as you continue to plan and set realistic goals, and as long as you continue to strive toward creative excellence, all that remains is to acquire business acumen.

Artisan Turned Manager

Being a self-employed artisan has its advantages and disadvantages. One important advantage is that you have the greatest possible amount of control over the business you're involved in when you're the one who's running it. The time and energy required to manage your business, however, are time and energy not devoted to the aspect we artisans enjoy most: the creative process.

A fact you must face at the outset, before you carry this idea of running your own business any further, is that as a self-employed artisan, you will probably spend considerably less time creating craft items than you will seeing to all the business-management chores and paperwork. The best you can hope and plan for is that your work will be equally divided between the creative process and management. If you don't have a taste for management, get a job, or keep the one you have.

If you work for someone else, you need only be good at the job for which you were hired. As the owner/manager of a home-based craft business, however, you will not only have to demonstrate creative expertise, but you will also have to be a competent manager. In your own home-based business, you wear all the hats.

Quick Quiz for the Home-Based Artisan

Before getting down to business, as it were, let's see if you've got the stuff to manage your own craft business. Answer *yes* or *no* to the following questions.

	Yes	No
1. Are you a self-starter?	___	___
2. Are you willing to work harder and longer than you ever imagined?	___	___
3. Do you work well without supervision?	___	___
4. Do you work well under pressure?	___	___
5. Are you able to organize details?	___	___
6. Can you take charge of projects and see them through to completion?	___	___
7. Do you have an independent nature?	___	___
8. Do you consider yourself well disciplined?	___	___
9. Are you willing to make sacrifices to succeed?	___	___
10. Do you consider honesty important in business?	___	___
11. Do you assume all your business dealings will be with honest people?	___	___
12. Do you mind seeing to menial chores?	___	___
13. Do you work best as a team member?	___	___
14. Are you a procrastinator?	___	___
15. Do you think work has to be fun?	___	___
16. Are you a creative person?	___	___
17. Can you be stern with people who owe you money?	___	___
18. Do you consider it necessary to meet or beat all deadlines?	___	___
19. Do you have a firm grasp of the basics of your chosen craft(s)?	___	___
20. Do you own sufficient and adequate craft-making equipment?	___	___

	Yes	No
21. Do you own as much craft-making equipment as you'll ever need?	——	——
22. Do you know as much about crafts as you'll ever need to know?	——	——
23. Is the camaraderie of coworkers necessary?	——	——
24. Do you feel that strict follow-up procedures are a waste of time?	——	——
25. Are peer recognition and praise essential to your success and happiness?	——	——

If you answered *yes* to questions 1 through 10, *no* to 11 through 15, *yes* to 16 through 20, and *no* to 21 through 25, why aren't you already running your own home-based craft business?

Don't fret if you have some *yes* answers where *no* answers belong, or vice versa. This test was designed to provide a quick self-evaluation and to call to your attention some of the realities of being a self-employed artisan and manager. You may have discovered one weakness or several, areas you need to work on, or attitudes that need adjusting.

Chapter Two

Working Out of Your Home

During much of the twentieth century, the trend for most Americans was to live in one place and work in another. In recent years, however, increasing numbers of people have moved back to their homes to do business. Studies by the U.S. Small Business Administration indicated that more than 400,000 home-based businesses were launched in 1985. That figure has since soared to more than one million new home-based businesses each year.

Several technological advancements have combined to allow people the increased freedom of working at home. Certainly, the development of the personal computer must head the list. Reinforcing the computer revolution were the establishment of computer database services, modems for computer-to-computer communication, global communication networks, satellite communication, improvements in telecommunications equipment and telephone services, fiber-optics technology, and the introduction of modern facsimile (fax) machines and fax modems. And now we have an information superhighway that has even further revolutionized the way global cartels, major corporations, small businesses, and individual entrepreneurs communicate, interact, and conduct their business.

Augmenting all these technological advances was the establishment of nationwide networks of rapid delivery and courier services. The U.S. Postal Service offers Express Mail overnight delivery to most destinations within the United States. United Parcel Service guarantees next-day delivery with its "Red Label" service and second-day delivery of the cheaper "Blue Label" parcels. Similar services are available at competitive prices from other companies, such as FedEx. It's now possible to send a letter, proposal, price sheet, report, manuscript, or stack of documents coast to coast faster than it took to get a document across town thirty years ago.

The attraction of working at home enticed many of us to go into business for ourselves. Working where we live allows us to avoid long, time-wasting commutes and reduces wear and tear on our vehicles. We're able to escape the hassles of office politics and personality conflicts with bosses and peers. We can dodge all the nonproductive meetings and work at our own improved pace. We can also arrange flexible schedules to accommodate a variety of needs.

The Pros and Cons of Self-Employment

For most of us who have been in business a while, the advantages of home-based self-employment far outweigh the disadvantages. You ought to know at the outset, though, that some people just don't take to this kind of life. So approach your business cautiously and weigh the options carefully.

I get the impression from people I talk to that the two qualities most people either think or fear they lack are self-motivation and self-discipline. These two attributes work hand in hand and are essential to the success of any home-based business, but they are realities you simply must face, not fears that should put you off unnecessarily. Of course, you must be motivated. Of course, you must be disciplined. But so must you be to hold a job, to get to work on time, to show up for appointments, to take responsibility for projects, to see to family business, to be a dependable person, to be a good friend.

The move from passenger to pilot can seem a quantum leap, but it needn't be frightening. You'll have to reach inside yourself to find the required character traits, but outside influences may be even greater motivators. When people ask me how I can get up every morning and go to work without giving in to the temptation to sleep in or take the day off and go fishing, I tell them it's easy: I have a natural aversion to poverty, hunger, and failure.

All of us are tempted from time to time, and on rare occasions we even give in. It's human nature, and there's nothing wrong with that. What you can't afford to do, however, is to make a habit of succumbing to all the diversions and thereby jeopardize deadlines and other commitments. To do so is to risk your reputation—indeed, your business.

If sleeping in or taking a day or afternoon off might cause you to miss a deadline, then don't do it. If, on the other hand, you've been working hard and a little time off will do no harm, then the decision is up to you. Keep in mind, though, that when you miss a morning, an afternoon, or an entire day, all your business activities screech to a halt; the work won't get done in your absence. You might have to put in some evenings or weekend time to catch up. So every time you're tempted, ask yourself if it's worth it.

The All-Collar Worker

At a conference I attended several years ago, an economist talked about blue-collar and white-collar workers, then told the audience about no-collar workers. "I'm talking about people who wear T-shirts or sweatshirts, Levi's, and running shoes," he said. "They work at home, and they represent the fastest-growing segment of the workforce."

He was referring to the millions of Americans who work full time from their homes. Some are home-based employees of corporations, while the rest are in business for themselves.

Although his facts and figures were interesting, his labeling was all wrong. In our home-based businesses, each of us runs the gamut from chief executive to laborer. I make all the important administrative and creative decisions in my business, but I also order the office supplies, make the coffee, vacuum the carpet, sweep up the shop, dust the filing cabinets and bookshelves, put off the filing, and wish someone would wash the windows. If anything, I'm an all-collar worker.

No More Nine-to-Five Grind

Many persons who aspire to the independence of running a home-based business dream of the day when they can chuck the daily routine: no more Monday-through-Friday, nine-to-five grind. That's true. Your home-based craft business will probably require a Monday-through-Saturday schedule, with plenty of Sundays thrown in. Instead of slugging away from nine to five, you'll probably be hard at it from six to six and might have to work some evenings to keep up.

No More Bosses

Similarly, those who think being their own boss is the greatest benefit of being self-employed are in for some surprises. The idea of any craft business is to have customers, and plenty of them. Your job is to please your customers. In a sense, then, every customer is your boss. Depending on the nature of your business, you might have orders to fill, commissions to complete, fairs and exhibits to attend—in other words, a life as full of deadlines as any job you may have had before starting your own business.

So if you are thinking of going into business because you don't like following your boss's orders or you hate the pressure of incessant deadlines, you're doing it for the wrong reasons. As a self-employed artisan, you must honor your commitments to countless people, and you must meet their deadlines. To do otherwise is to court peril.

Isolation—Curse or Blessing?

Isolation is also something every home-based artisan must deal with. Oddly, the reality of it comes as a surprise to many people who decide to run businesses from their homes. Some are truly distraught by being cut off from the daily interaction with others, particularly those who leave busy jobs where isolation is rare or nonexistent. The rest of us revel in the solitude and the high level of productivity it fosters.

If most of your business is local, you will come in contact with more people than if the bulk of your work is for distant clients. Even in the latter case, you'll need to stay in touch with people by phone, mail, e-mail, and through the occasional business trip, trade show, association meeting, or craft fair.

If your craft business is one that requires meetings with clients, you might consider luncheon meetings as a way of getting away from home for an hour or so. This can be a refreshing diversion if you don't mind dividing your workday to allow it. Breakfast meetings can be a good alternative for people who don't like to break up their workdays.

Artisans who sell their products mainly at craft fairs and arts-and-crafts exhibits rarely get to know their customers. Even if you sell regularly to local or regional galleries and gift shops, most of your clients will probably remain casual acquaintances whom you're not inclined to lunch with. So if you feel the need to get away from your home or to engage in conversation, take a lunch break with a friend or spouse. You might even plan these luncheons to be regular, if not frequent, diversions.

Two self-employed friends of mine make it a point to have lunch together once or twice a month as a way of getting out of the house and having a conversation with someone who's not a customer or family member. They've gone so far as to set up a lunch fund to which each contributes. That way, no one's responsible for the tab or tip, and they feel as if neither has to pay for lunch. Little games like this tend to open pressure valves and help make running a business more enjoyable.

Setting Up Your Business Space

One of the first orders of business is to plan, design, and set up your work space. This is a matter of both logistics and legalities. Your business will require a certain amount of space. Your home may or may not impose space restrictions on your business. In order to qualify as a legitimate business for tax purposes, the space you set aside will have to meet certain criteria. (See Chapter 7 under "Using Your Home as a Business.")

The advantages of converting part of your home to a work space far outweigh the alternative, which is to rent or lease business space. Typically, commercial space rents for at least $2.00 a square foot per month. You won't burn out any brain cells calculating the $300 a month you'll save by converting a 10-by-15-foot spare room into a home office instead of renting an office downtown.

Just to rent the commercial equivalent of my office, studio, darkroom, and workshop would cost me more than $2,300 a month, or nearly four times my monthly mortgage payment. What's more, I get an annual tax deduction for that part of my home devoted entirely to the operation of my business.

How and where you go about setting up your work space is entirely up to you and depends largely on the space available and how you intend to operate. Obviously, if your business is solely devoted to needlecraft, you won't need a big workshop full of expensive woodworking tools. If you're both an artist and an artisan, perhaps one room will serve as both studio and workshop. If your office is big enough, it might also double as a studio or workroom. A large closet can become a storeroom. You can convert a garage or outbuilding into a warehouse.

Every home-based entrepreneur, however, needs a place to conduct business: to see to correspondence, accounts payable, accounts receivable, the endless flow of paperwork, and all the other business chores. Whether this turns out to be one end of the dining-room table, a desk in a corner of a bedroom, or a full-fledged home office depends on what you need and what's available.

One of the beauties of the home-based craft business is that you can start small. Even if your chosen craft is relatively expensive, you probably won't need as much equipment and materials as you would in another kind of business. Consequently, your start-up costs can be comparatively low. Depending on what you already own and how good you are at scrounging and improvising, you should be able to get into business for somewhere between a few hundred and a few thousand dollars—certainly less than five thousand.

As mentioned previously, you need to set up some sort of office space, and while there's nothing wrong with using part of another room in your home, you may not claim that space as a home office when you file your tax return. Any space you set up in your home for the purpose of running a business must be used *regularly* and *exclusively* for that business if you are going to claim a deduction for it. That means it must be a separate room or rooms. If you don't have separate facilities available, so be it.

If you can, though, try to convert any available rooms, add on, or plan for the additional space the next time you move or build. It's better not only for tax purposes, but also for doing business and keeping your business and personal life separate. You will have a discrete, clearly defined place to go to work, to conduct business, and, perhaps most important, to leave at the end of the workday.

As in any other planning operation, you need to put this information on paper. You should write out your wants and needs and sketch out floor plans that will accommodate your physical requirements.

You can operate a craft business from any kind of dwelling. Since my part-time beginnings, I have run my business from an apartment, two log cabins, a town house, a rental house, and finally from the house I live in now, which was designed to include comfortable living quarters on one level and my business complex on the other.

When I started my business, my wife and I lived in a two-bedroom apartment. I was able to set up one bedroom as my office and makeshift studio. Although I was able to design woodworking projects in the comfort of my office/studio, I had to see to the labor outdoors, where I set up a temporary workbench with a slab of plywood on two sawhorses.

We had a similar situation at the town house we rented when we moved to the Oregon coast. There, though, a private patio served as my outdoor workshop. When it rained, I moved my work to the kitchen. Adjacent to the kitchen and next to the sliding door to the patio was a large closet with bifold doors, which I converted into a compact workshop and storage area.

One of the two bedrooms on the second floor of the town house served as my office and studio. It was a separate room that I used exclusively and regularly for business purposes and was therefore deductible as a home office. The patio and kitchen, however, were temporary work spaces, not used exclusively for business purposes, so they did not qualify for any kind of deduction.

I did not take a deduction for the large closet I had converted, for which I can only plead stupidity. For some reason, it never occurred to me that I could—after all, it was just a closet. It was not functioning as a closet, however. It was a separate room, with doors closing it off from other rooms. I used it exclusively and regularly for business purposes. So it qualified for a legitimate deduction I failed to take. Don't make the same kind of mistake.

There never seems to be enough storage room, so plan accordingly. When we moved into the town house, I got along fine for about a year, but then I had to rent additional storage space. When we built the house we now occupy, we planned carefully and thought we'd never run out of space. We have used up all that space, however, and have once again had to rent a storage unit to house the overflow.

In planning the physical structure of your business, pay close attention to your equipment requirements. List your immediate needs for each aspect of your business and note how you intend to fill them. You might also list your midrange and long-term needs. If you answered the series of ten questions near the beginning of Chapter 1, you have already made such a list in response to question 5. Following are some hints that may help you in this process.

The Home Office

The bare essentials for any home office include a desk, chair, filing cabinet, wastebasket, telephone, and computer with appropriate software. You will probably want a bookcase or bookshelves, and perhaps a storage cabinet of some sort. Most of us need some kind of calculator; I have several small ones stashed here and there and a larger printing calculator on my desk for use in my bookkeeping and accounting chores. To keep track of important names, addresses, and phone numbers, you should have some sort of index—at least an address book, but better yet, a Rolodex file, or computer software that lets you store and retrieve such information electronically. You'll need a postage scale and at least three file trays or baskets: *In, Pending,* and *Out.* You'll probably find that three aren't nearly enough.

The necessary office tools include pens, pencils, felt-tip markers, ruler, stapler, staple remover, and scissors. You will want at least one tape dispenser; I keep two on my desk: one for transparent tape, one for removable transparent tape.

Required office materials vary from one business to another but certainly include assorted paper products, staples, paper clips, spring clips, adhesive tapes, mailing and shipping labels, printer and copier cartridges, rubber bands, batteries, and file folders.

Paper products I use include scratch pads, Post-it notes, letter-size ruled pads, printer and copier paper, graph paper, letterhead stationery and envelopes, business cards, 3-by-5-inch index cards, self-adhesive labels in assorted sizes, chipboard and cardboard stiffeners (for protecting photographs and artwork in the mail), large mailing envelopes in different sizes, padded mailers, and various printed forms.

You will eventually discover other tools and materials that, while not indispensable, certainly save time, money, effort, or all three. For example, I keep a three-hole punch on my desk and an assortment of rubber stamps.

I use a lot of batteries to power electronic photography equipment, flashlights, tape recorders, calculators, and other gadgets. I switched from alkaline to the rechargeable nickel-cadmium batteries some years ago, because they seldom need replacing, save money, and are kinder to the environment when properly discarded. So I keep two battery chargers busy.

If not an immediate need, a phone-answering machine should at least get high-priority listing. These machines are available with a wide range of feature options and prices to match. When I bought mine several years ago, I wondered if I would ever need all its bells and whistles. I doubted the worth of a fifty-number memory dialer and considered the speakerphone only marginally useful.

I was wrong. I've managed to fill all fifty slots in the memory dialer, and the speakerphone alone is worth the price of the entire machine for the time it saves. Anyone working with computers knows that phoning a toll-free technical-support number is infuriatingly time consuming. There are never enough technicians to handle all the calls, so we wait. And wait. And wait. During one call I spent forty-three minutes on hold. By switching on the speakerphone, however, I was able to get on with my work while holding my place in line. This feature also saves time when I place orders or see to other business via toll-free numbers and am put on hold.

Just as you should plan for more storage space and phone features than you think you'll need, try to design as much horizontal working surface as possible into your home office. Desktops are never large enough, and they act like magnets for clutter. So plan for more surface space than a single desk offers, perhaps with the addition of a worktable, a credenza, or even a second desk.

I have two desks in my office. A conventional desk stands in the middle of the room, and another behind it functions as a computer station. Other furniture and fixtures in my office include two-drawer and four-drawer filing cabinets, a wall of bookshelves, an AM-FM stereo, and a cuckoo clock for company—birds of a feather, I guess.

The Home Studio

A studio is many things to many people and can be anything you want to make it. It's probably the most variable room of all among home-based artists and artisans. You may not need one at all, but if you do, you must determine how you will use it in order to know how much space you need and how you will furnish it. My studio would be more than some people might need but woefully inadequate for others.

I knew when I designed my work complex that I needed a fair-sized multipurpose room, which, for lack of a better name, I called my studio. It's a rectangular room, 13 by 18 feet. One end of it functions as a photography studio, but the room does much more than that. Four-drawer filing cabinets line one wall, and floor-to-ceiling bookshelves run the length of two others. So this is also my research and reference library.

Permanent furniture includes a desk, a chair, and a large worktable. Atop the desk are dozens of labeled file trays that initially sort the mountain of paperwork associated with running my business. So the studio is also where I do most of my filing.

Woodworking is a major part of my business, but I also do a good bit of picture framing. Although I build and finish frames in my workshop, I see to the rest of the framing process in my studio, simply because framing requires a relatively dust-free environment, which no woodworking shop provides.

Before we built the house we currently occupy, my studio and office were in the same room, and I got along adequately with that arrangement. As my business grew, I soon realized that I would need much more space than any single room might provide, and that was my motivation for having separate office and studio/library facilities.

The Home Workshop

A workshop is another room you may or may not need, depending on the kind of craft you create. This is a province for the messy crafts, and you might call this work space a workshop, workroom, or studio. In my case, it's clearly a workshop, full of hand tools, portable and stationary power tools, and woodworking materials.

My next-door neighbor is a woodcarver who works in his garage, which is also full of hand tools, portable and stationary power tools, and woodworking materials. He calls his work space a studio, and I wouldn't quibble with that nomenclature. He's more artist than artisan, and I'm the opposite. My shop and his studio are similar because of the medium we work in and the fact that each of us regularly dabbles in the other's realm.

My shop is 24 by 24 feet and is comfortable and adequate for creating a great variety of woodcraft projects. Storage has become a problem in recent years. Consequently, in addition to renting storage space, I'm gradually reorganizing my work complex to relieve the burden that has befallen both my shop and studio.

Keep this in mind as you design your own work space. Try to allow for more room than you think you'll need. As your business prospers and grows, however, your work space will begin bulging at the seams. That may be a good time to reassess your needs and possibly redesign and expand your business space.

The Home Warehouse

As I mentioned earlier, you're going to need storage space, and plenty of it—probably more than you think—and at times you may need more than usual. Building inventory to prepare for the upcoming tourist season or Christmas-shopping season can put a strain on your storage facilities, as can stockpiling for an arts-and-crafts fair.

Part of your workshop or studio may suffice. You might temporarily have to use an attic or another room in your house, but remember, if you don't use that room regularly and exclusively for business purposes, it is not eligible for a tax deduction.

Another option is to rent or lease storage space temporarily at one of the mini–storage facilities available in most communities. If you use this space exclusively for storing your products and other business-related items, you can deduct the rent as a business expense.

If you regularly travel the craft-fair and trade-show circuits and find you have a relatively permanent problem with storing inventory, you should consider converting another room, adding on, or putting up a separate facility to function as a permanent home-business warehouse.

Handling Growth

There's nothing wrong with modest beginnings. In fact, I'd recommend you start small. But you must plan to succeed, which means you must plan to expand, perhaps several times, and eventually to limit or curtail expansion. In short, you must control the growth of your business.

If you operate your craft business intelligently and aggressively, it will grow—most rapidly during the first few years. You could also experience rapid growth whenever you branch out into another craft area. You must pace that growth according to your abilities, resources, and available space.

Eventually, you will be getting all the business you can handle, at which time you must decide whether to level off or continue expanding. This is not as easy a decision as it might first appear.

Many entrepreneurs equate growth with success and insist that in order to succeed a business must grow, which is true to some extent. It is, indeed, important for a business to grow during its formative years. It can be dangerous, however, to extend the growth notion too far: to think that the faster a business grows, the more successful it will be; or to believe that if a business doesn't continue to grow, it is destined to fail.

It is possible to grow too fast—that is, to take on more than you can handle. If prices quoted to your clients or customers are based on a business run by one person, you can get into serious trouble if you must hire help or farm out work to others to honor your commitments and meet deadlines. Not only might this reduce or even eliminate your profits, but it can also eat into your operating capital. Your dilemma is that you must either break your promises and miss deadlines or spend extra money to get the work done on time. You can't operate that way and expect to stay in business.

Even with proper planning and managed growth, you will eventually reach a saturation point. That's when you'll have to decide whether to level off or hire help.

Working with Others

Sometimes the promise of high profits can cloud one's vision and impair judgment. There's nothing wrong with providing jobs for others, but you must keep in mind why you wanted your own home-based craft business in the first place. Was it to build an empire, or was it to provide yourself with a satisfying career and a comfortable income? In case of the former, you must be willing and able to accept the hassles and responsibilities that come with empire building. If you're among the latter group, you must know how to manage and curtail growth and how to handle potential growth problems.

As your business grows, you will discover that there are times when seven days aren't enough to get the week's work done. A number of factors can contribute to scheduling problems and the need for careful scrutiny of your business's labor requirements.

- *Seasonal aspects.* You might find that there are times of the year when you have more work than you can handle. The holiday season, for example—from October through Christmas Eve—is a time of high-volume sales for most crafts. Mother's Day and Father's Day are other peak times for craft gifts. Where I live, the tourist season is important.
- *Rush orders.* You won't be in business long before you discover that few customers

and clients plan ahead. Everybody, it seems, needs it yesterday. Instead of paying attention to inventory and placing timely orders, even clients who should know better will end up phoning you only when they've run out of your products.

- *Special projects.* From time to time you will probably land jobs or be commissioned to do work outside of or in addition to your usual business. Often these can be lucrative projects that you can't afford to turn down. Indeed, you might pursue or even initiate them yourself. As well as they may pay, they can put additional demands on your business that call for extraordinary measures.

- *Accumulated chores.* Dealing with all the above problems will force you to set priorities and to put off low-priority tasks until time permits you to address them. These lesser jobs can eventually grow into major responsibilities that cry for immediate attention.

When faced with these or similar circumstances, you have several choices. Enlisting the help of a family member could be the simplest solution, but this isn't always possible. In my own business, my wife is a great helpmate. But she has her own full-time career, so she isn't available during the course of a normal workweek.

If you need help with your work and, for one reason or another, no one in your family can come to your aid, you might have to consider hiring help. Your alternatives are to hire personnel on your own or to work with a local employment service.

Often, hiring help only adds to your burdens, so I recommend you do this only as a last resort. You'll probably need to advertise. Then you'll have to screen and interview prospective employees. In order to attract competent applicants, you'll have to offer a competitive wage and certain fringe benefits.

State and federal regulations make hiring personnel difficult, expensive, and time consuming. You must pay for unemployment insurance, Social Security, and workers' compensation. You're responsible for deducting Social Security taxes as well as federal, state, and local income taxes from an employee's pay and submitting the deducted funds to the various agencies with all the appropriate forms.

On top of all that, you'll have to pay for a certain amount of nonproduction: holidays, sick days, personal days, and vacation time. And you will probably be responsible for some kind of health insurance. The paperwork for all this can be a nightmare, and the cost can soar to an amount equivalent to 40 to 45 percent of the employee's pay. In other words, if you pay a full-time employee $10 an hour, or $400 a week, your actual costs will be in the neighborhood of $14.50 an hour, or $580 a week.

After your business's workload subsides or returns to normal, you'll have to lay off anyone you've hired. This can be a depressing duty for you and certainly an unhappy event for the employee. What's more, it can increase premiums for unemployment compensation insurance.

Hiring Temporary Help

You'll probably be far better off hiring temporary help through an employment service, not to be confused with an employment agency. Both are companies that provide workers for other businesses. The employment service tests, screens, hires, and trains the workers; pays their salaries; provides all their benefits; makes all the necessary payroll deductions; and sees to all the paperwork.

Well before you have an actual need, you should find out what sort of temporary help is available in your locale. Check with the local chamber of commerce or Small Business Development Center. Look in the Yellow Pages under such headings as "Employee Leasing," "Employment—Temporary," and "Employment Contractors—Temporary Help."

Most such companies have an employee pool with a wide range of skills in a variety of fields. Most have clerical help and skilled office workers available, and some have people competent in certain specialty areas.

When you use an employment service, you pay an hourly rate to the service, which then pays the employee and keeps a portion for the service. The rate you pay obviously must be higher than what you will pay to an employee you hire yourself but will probably work out to be a better deal for you in the final analysis.

For example, if the employment service charges you $15 an hour for the kind of employee you could have hired directly for $10 an hour, this might seem exorbitant at first glance. Consider, however, that your $10-an-hour employee will actually cost you $14.50 an hour. So in essence, you end up paying a mere 50 cents an hour to avoid all the time-consuming chores and paperwork associated with advertising for, interviewing, screening, training, and paying an employee.

Independent Contractors

An alternative to hiring help is to use the services of an independent contractor—someone who, like you, is self-employed and works by the job or by the hour, under contract. You and the contractor agree in writing to what the job entails and how much you will pay. The contractor is then responsible for doing the work as stipulated, paying self-employment and income taxes, and filing the necessary forms.

If you use independent contractors in your work, there is one form you might have to file. The Internal Revenue Service requires you to file a Form 1099-MISC for any independent contractor you pay more than $600 during the tax year.

You can advertise for an independent contractor in a local newspaper's classified section, or you can try to find someone through other sources. Put the word out at local galleries, gift shops, and stores that sell arts-and-crafts supplies. Other good sources include arts-and-crafts schools, some technical schools, and any nearby college or university with an art department, especially one offering courses in applied arts.

You can hire an independent contractor for any job for which you might otherwise hire an employee. The big difference is that you can avoid most of the headaches and nuisances associated with being an employer.

You can also hire independent contractors for jobs you would otherwise do yourself—either in your business or in your home. When you hire a plumber or an electrician, you're hiring an independent contractor, and either the contractor or one of his employees will take care of the job. If you know how to do such work yourself, you can save money. Some contractors, however, might save you money in the long run by freeing you from the task and thereby allowing you to make more money, hour for hour, than you have to pay the contractor. And there may be some jobs you simply don't want to do.

If a light switch or electrical outlet needs replacing, I'm not about to hire an electrician who will charge me $45 (probably much higher elsewhere, especially in big cities) when I can buy the fixture for less than $5.00 and do the job in five minutes.

On the other hand, if I can hire an independent contractor for jobs I hate doing, for less than I can make during the time the jobs take, hiring the contractor makes good sense. Recently, I had a list of repair and maintenance jobs I gave to an independent contractor. All were tasks I've normally taken care of over the years—such as cleaning eaves, replacing soffit-vent screens, cleaning the roof and skylights, and replacing broken chimney guy wires—but they would have taken me two full weekends, precious free time I didn't want to give up. The handyman I hired did all the jobs in three days and charged me $280, which was far less than I made in those three days.

As my business has grown, my time has become more precious to me and has certainly increased in monetary value. Recently, my wife and I have been examining many of the chores we've customarily done ourselves with an eye toward hiring others to do them, to allow us either more free time or more productive time. You should do the same.

I long ago gave up the time-consuming and backbreaking job of cleaning our carpeting. Carpet-cleaning services have much better equipment than I can rent, and they get the work done in half the time it would take me.

Another independent contractor we hire regularly works as an auto detailer. I know how to detail a vehicle, but I can no longer justify doing it myself; nor do I have the patience to do as complete a job as a good detailer will do. I have my business vehicle and our family vehicle detailed each spring and fall. The detailer picks up the vehicle at my house in the morning and returns it by day's end. He thoroughly cleans it inside and out, including the engine, tires, wheels, and undercarriage. He polishes and buffs the body, then waxes and buffs it. He charges $135 for a job that would take me all day.

You might be able to do a passable job of painting your house, but you should ask yourself some questions first:

- Do you know how to properly clean and prepare the surface you intend to paint?
- Do you know what kind of primer and paint you will need?
- Will you be able to do as good a job as a professional painting contractor?
- Do you really want to do the job yourself?
- How long will the entire job take you?
- How much can you make working the same amount of time at your craft business?

If you run through this little exercise for all the various repair and maintenance chores you normally do yourself, you'll soon find some that are better left to independent contractors. As your business grows and prospers, you'll find more such jobs that you'll gladly hire out.

A warning is in order here, however. Be careful to avoid running afoul of IRS regulations when hiring independent contractors to help in your business. Remember, an independent contractor is self-employed and sells products or services to others. An agent who represents you, sells your work at trade shows or to shops and galleries, and keeps a percentage of the sale price as a commission qualifies as an independent contractor. A computer consultant you hire to help set up a system and perform other services as required is an independent contractor.

If you hire people to help produce craft items, however, the IRS will probably consider them employees if they are following procedures you have developed for your products, even if they're not working on your premises.

On the other hand, I know of two woodworkers who regularly hire artists as independent contractors to paint scenes on their woodcraft items. I know cabinetmakers who sometimes hire wood-carvers as independent contractors to carve door and drawer panels. The big difference here is that the artists and carvers are allowed the artistic freedom to paint and carve their own scenes and impressions without following someone else's step-by-step procedures.

The best advice I can offer is to describe in writing how you intend to hire and occupy independent contractors, and allow a local IRS agent to review your plan and advise you. Get the agent's response in writing or get a notation on your plan signed and dated. If local agents are reluctant, you can request an official ruling in writing from the Internal Revenue Service in Washington, D.C.

Collaborating

Collaboration is another way to get help on jobs without hiring employees. In a collaboration you work with one or more other persons to complete a project. For example, you might work with another artisan or artist on a commission or a specific job. You might also collaborate regularly on an entire line of products.

You can handle such informal partnerships in a number of ways. Where the work of each party is about equal, you can equally split costs and profits. You can hire a collaborator at that person's hourly or daily rate or on a per-piece basis. You can even work out a swap arrangement whereby you and your collaborator swap services and then sell your own products individually.

Separating Business Life from Personal Life

I have read that it's impossible for the home-based entrepreneur to keep business life and personal life separate. To the extent that no business or job can be kept entirely isolated from personal and family affairs, I would agree. But it's essential for the success of your business and the well-being of your personal life that you make every effort to keep the two distinct and apart.

If you have a family, your home-based business is going to affect it in some way, and vice versa. If your business is only in the preliminary planning stages, waste no time in bringing certain family members on board and making clear to them what your plans are and how they might affect family life. A spouse should be part of your planning from the start. You may want to postpone discussing the venture with young children until you're ready to launch the business, but you should talk with older children early on.

Moreover, you must make it clear to your family, friends, and neighbors that although you will be working at home in your new business, you are indeed working, and during work hours you are not available for chores, baby-sitting, ball playing, shopping, shuttle service, or anything else not related to your craft business.

For some baffling reason, people tend to think that a person who works at home isn't really working. Consequently, you can count on them to try to impose on you in every imaginable way. Friends, neighbors, and even family members will think nothing of phoning or dropping in during business hours just to chat, when they would never dream of doing such a thing to a chef, a physician, a teacher, or an auto mechanic who works away from home.

Sometimes home-based entrepreneurs get what they ask for—no respect. I've heard of some who delight in the fact that they're able to work at home all day in robe and slippers. I can't imagine taking my business seriously, or expecting others to, while lounging around all day in bed clothing. I certainly can't entertain or meet with clients so attired. And what are drop-ins and coffee klatchers to think if I greet them at the door in pajamas and try to convince them I'm busy?

Of course, I might catch up on paperwork late at night in the bedroom. I often see to early-morning phone calls during my first cup of coffee, before I've showered and donned my work duds. When it's time for business, however, I'm dressed for it.

It's also important for your business image and peace of mind that you establish a business routine. You must have operating days and hours, and you must make these known to family, friends, and neighbors. Otherwise, they'll be all too quick to assume you're not really working.

Chapter Three
Financial Planning

In the broadest sense, the operation of any business can be divided into two basic categories: the management of money and the management of time. Although the two are inextricably intertwined, you should first expend your efforts toward planning and managing financial matters.

For most people, starting a new business involves a great deal of guesswork. I suspect that's one reason so many small businesses soon end up in financial difficulty. The home-based artisan has the distinct advantage of being able to operate part time before starting a full-time business. The ability to analyze revenues and expenditures from the part-time business and extrapolate them to reflect full-time operation removes much of the speculation and makes financial planning more accurate and management much easier.

Even if you start your business on a part-time basis, however, you must not treat it as a hobby. I suspect that most artisans who decide to start a craft business began as serious amateurs who sold enough work to buy craft equipment and materials and offset the costs of their hobby. A business—part time or full time—must do more than that. It must generate sufficient revenue to cover expenditures *and make a profit*.

I can't stress enough the importance of being cost conscious and ever vigilant against rising costs. Cutting and containing costs must be a constant concern from the onset—even before you establish your business.

It's never too soon to begin planning and managing finances. If you're a hobbyist looking forward to turning your hobby into a business, begin keeping good records immediately. Learn exactly what everything costs and keep track of price increases. Conduct time studies to learn how long it takes you to do everything associated with your craft—and that includes management as well as the creative process. Then look for ways to cut costs and reduce time in all areas of your operation.

Start-up Costs

Before launching your business, you need to estimate what it will cost you. If you have kept good records of your amateur activities, estimating start-up costs should prove much easier. Nevertheless, it will still require some guessing, albeit guessing based on experience.

Even if you've never bought a new car and know little or nothing about cars, it's easy to learn approximately what such a purchase will cost. You simply do a little research, shop around, compare various makes and models, decide which features you need and which you don't, then negotiate the best deal possible.

Some new entrepreneurs expect determining the start-up costs of implementing a new business to be just as straightforward and clear-cut. Sadly, it is not. There is no way to calculate the exact costs of running a business until you're running it, and even then you must stay alert for potential surprises.

If that sounds like a risky catch-22, you have grasped the concept. However, you can greatly reduce the risks and improve the accuracy of your estimates by keeping good records as an amateur and then as a part-time professional.

You'll find that not all the projections, statements, and reports the accountants, consultants, and business writers insist we use are of equal value to all businesses; some are downright useless. Even those that are useful operating tools for running your business might prove to be of little or no value in the start-up process. Moreover, what works for one business or one manager might be less valuable to another. So find the tools that work for you.

In the pages that follow are some tips and tricks that should help steer you in the right direction and help you realistically estimate what the cost of starting your business might be.

Schedule of Estimated Start-up Costs

One document you will need is a schedule of estimated start-up costs.

This is a list of all the equipment, materials, supplies, and expenses associated with running your home-based craft business. Compiling the list will force you to dwell on impor-

Estimated Start-up Costs

1. Decorating and remodeling   _____

2. Furniture and fixtures   _____

3. Office equipment   _____

4. Craft equipment   _____

5. Vehicle   _____

6. Insurance   _____

7. Licenses and permits   _____

8. Legal and professional fees   _____

9. Office supplies and materials   _____

10. Craft supplies and materials   _____

11. Stationery and business cards   _____

12. Advertising   _____

13. Unexpected expenses   _____

Total Estimated Start-up Costs   _____

tant details you might otherwise ignore, such as what insurance will cost, how much raw material you'll have to stock, what your phone and utilities will cost—in short, how expensive this business is going to be. The total of all these costs will be the start-up target you'll need to aim for as you plan your business.

Most of the business guides I've reviewed recommend that new entrepreneurs have at least three months' operating capital before launching a new business, and few mention anything about the owner's salary. You will certainly want to include your salary as part of any start-up projection you make. What's more, you ought to have more backing you than a mere three months' worth of funding for a full-time business.

I ran my business part time until I had a year's salary and expenses in the bank, and all the while I was investing in and upgrading equipment. By the time I was ready to go full time, my business was in good shape, and I was able to run it without many financial worries. I suggest you take a similar route and make sure you have at least six months' salary and operating capital backing you.

Opening Bank Accounts

I've read a number of publications that insist the first thing an entrepreneur must do is head for a bank and open a business checking account. The authors warn that you must never use a personal checking account for business purposes. One reason given is that business and personal accounts must be kept separate for bookkeeping and tax purposes. Another is that vendors and others you deal with won't think much of you if you pay with personal checks. What utter nonsense!

So what is the home-based entrepreneur with two separate accounts to do at bill-paying time? Write personal checks for the home or personal portion of the electric bill and auto insurance, then write business checks for the business portions? What a bookkeeper's nightmare that would be.

As one who has been managing some kind of business—either mine or somebody else's—for more than thirty years, I can tell you that nobody is going to care one whit about being paid with a personal check instead of a business check, providing there are sufficient funds in the account. My wife and I have written more than 13,000 checks on the account we're now using. A creditor is going to worry a lot less about my personal check #13875 than business check #11 from some outfit that's been operating for about a month.

More than one publication suggests that aspiring entrepreneurs can shake the onus of the obviously new business checking account by ordering checks that begin with higher numbers. In other words, instead of a sequential check-numbering system that begins with check #1 or #101, you should direct the printer to start with #1001 and put something over on suppliers and others whose products and services you purchase. Anyone who thinks this ruse has escaped the attention of vendors and their credit managers is naive. What's more, credit managers don't set up new accounts until they've run credit investigations. So credit will be extended to you before anyone has seen the color of your money.

If you already have a personal checking account, use it. If not, set one up. If you prefer a business checking account, that's all right too, but don't establish one for the wrong reasons.

I do recommend that you set up a separate business savings account rather than use a personal savings account for business. The extra account won't cost you anything and will make it easy to keep business funds separate. An alternative is to skip the business savings account and open an interest-bearing checking account for your business. Visit a number of banks and find out what they offer. Then establish the kind of account that provides the most and costs the least.

My wife and I had a joint checking account that I also used for business for eighteen years. I had a savings account for my business at the same bank for just as long. We also have a personal savings account at another bank. Both banks have branches less than a mile from our home, which is one of the reasons we chose them.

In 1993 we closed the checking and business savings accounts and opened new accounts at the bank where we have our personal savings account. The bank we'd done business with since 1975 kept boosting service charges and had begun charging for services that used to be free. A little gouge here, a little gouge there, and before long the accounts were costing us far more than they should. When the bank started charging me for deposit slips, I decided it was time to take our business elsewhere. The move has saved us more than $200 a year.

Don't let the cost of an account, however, be your sole guide. Consider the importance of convenience and simplicity. For example, by shopping around, you will probably discover that some banks offer lower monthly service charges than others, and a few might have no service charges at all. But you must also weigh the value of conveniences, such as proximity to your home, parking, and drive-up windows. If you save a dollar a month on service charges only to spend thirty extra minutes a week driving to and from the bank, you're wasting two hours a month and losing money in the process. Time is money in any business, and it pays to manage both wisely.

The Personal Financial Statement

Do you know what you're worth? Your creditors may want to know, and any institution you approach for a long-term loan certainly will. To answer the question, you should prepare a *personal financial statement,* also known as a *statement of financial condition,* or *statement of net worth.*

This is a relatively simple form with two columns. To prepare it, start by creating a form with your name, address, and phone number centered at the top of the page.

In the left column list all your assets: cash, checking accounts, savings accounts, real

Personal Financial Statement

Name _____

Address _____

_____

Phone _____

Assets

Cash   _____

Checking Accounts _____

Savings Accounts   _____

Stocks   _____

Bonds   _____

Securities   _____

Real Estate   _____

Vehicles   _____

Accounts Receivable _____

Other Liquid Assets _____

Total Assets   _____

Liabilities

Accounts Payable   _____

Contracts Payable   _____

Notes Payable   _____

Taxes Payable   _____

Real Estate Loans   _____

Vehicle Loans   _____

Other Liabilities   _____

Total Liabilities   _____

Net Worth   _____
(assets minus liabilities)

estate, stocks, bonds, securities, and accounts receivable. Also list such assets as vehicles and equipment that have cash value after allowing for depreciation. When you add up this column, you'll arrive at a figure that represents your total assets.

In the right column list all your liabilities: accounts payable, contracts payable, notes payable, taxes payable, real estate loans, and anything else you owe. When you add up this column, you'll arrive at a figure that represents your total liabilities.

Subtract your total liabilities from your total assets and enter the result as your net worth.

Keep this statement on hand and update it periodically—at least every year. You will probably want to include it as part of your business plan (covered in Chapter 6).

Columnar Pads for Accounting and Bookkeeping

Accountants usually prepare various statements on columnar pads, the common sizes of which range from 8½ by 11 inches to 14 by 17 inches and include versions with three, four, six, eight, thirteen, and fourteen columns. Use whatever size and format of columnar pad works best for you, but be advised that the outsize, unwieldy pads are a nuisance to store.

For a number of reasons, I use one size and style of pad for all my accounting and bookkeeping: a vertical-format, four-column pad that measures 8½ by 11 inches. The format and standard letter size make such pads compatible with all my documents and files. They adapt handily to any application and fit neatly into a three-ring binder. I use them for making monthly, quarterly, annual, midrange, and long-range studies and projections as well as for all my income-tax records. What's more, I need only stock one size, so I order a dozen fifty-sheet pads at a time, thus markedly reducing my per-pad price.

Profit-and-Loss Projections and Reports

A profit-and-loss statement (often called a P&L) is an accounting document that measures or predicts your business's operation in terms of net sales or fees, less expenses and other costs, to create an accurate profit picture or reasonable profit prediction.

By definition, this document increases in management value with the life of the business, because its degree of accuracy depends on profit history. As defined, it's of marginal value for many start-up businesses.

You can make this a useful management tool if you will follow my recommendations and forgive my nagging. Keeping accurate records of all transactions during your amateur and part-time days and logging all the hours you spend working at your craft business will create a profit history you can use to make accurate projections for your full-time business.

The columnar pad commonly recommended for P&L statements is of horizontal format, with a 3-inch-wide column on the left and thirteen narrow columns across each page. To enter both estimated and actual figures for each month and the year-end totals, you can draw a vertical line down the center of each narrow column, creating twenty-six columns in all.

In my system, I forgo the ability to scan twenty-six columns on a single page, but I gain much more in the way of readability. Instead of a single statement that reflects estimated and actual figures, I prepare two separate documents: a P&L *projection* for estimated figures, and a P&L *report* for actual figures.

You will probably find that the calendar year works best as your business's fiscal year. Unless you start your business in January, though, the first months of operation will constitute a partial year. After that, however, you can do all projecting, calculating, bookkeeping, and reporting according to the standard January-to-December calendar.

If you use four-column pads, your profit-and-loss projection for the first full year will take up four pages. On the first page, create a column each for January, February, March, and First Quarter. Subsequent pages will reflect income and expenses for the remaining months and quarters.

The second-year P&L projection will require one page, with one column devoted to each quarter. Add a line at the bottom of the page for the year-end total. Add the totals for the four columns and enter the profit or loss as the year-end total.

For the long-range P&L projection, use one page with a column each for third-year, fourth-year, and fifth-year totals.

In the left column of the P&L projection, under *Revenue* list income from sale of services and merchandise on separate lines. Add the two, and enter a figure for *Total Revenue.*

Under *Cost of Goods Sold,* list amounts paid for materials and supplies, outside labor, shipping, and miscellaneous costs. Add this column, and enter a figure for *Total Cost of Goods Sold.*

Subtract *Total Cost of Goods Sold* from *Total Revenue* and enter the result as *Gross Income.*

Profit-and-Loss Projection/Report
(Estimated/Actual)

	January	February	March	First Quarter Totals
REVENUE				
Services	_____	_____	_____	_____
Merchandise sales	_____	_____	_____	_____
Total Revenue	_____	_____	_____	_____
COST OF GOODS SOLD				
Materials and supplies	_____	_____	_____	_____
Outside labor	_____	_____	_____	_____
Shipping	_____	_____	_____	_____
Miscellaneous	_____	_____	_____	_____
Total Cost of Goods Sold	_____	_____	_____	_____
Gross Profit	_____	_____	_____	_____
EXPENSES				
Wages/salaries	_____	_____	_____	_____
Payroll deductions	_____	_____	_____	_____
Advertising	_____	_____	_____	_____
Vehicle	_____	_____	_____	_____
Depreciation	_____	_____	_____	_____
Insurance	_____	_____	_____	_____
Interest paid	_____	_____	_____	_____
Legal & professional fees	_____	_____	_____	_____
Office supplies	_____	_____	_____	_____
Rent/lease	_____	_____	_____	_____
Repairs & maintenance	_____	_____	_____	_____
Supplies	_____	_____	_____	_____
Permits & licenses	_____	_____	_____	_____
Travel & entertainment	_____	_____	_____	_____
Utilities	_____	_____	_____	_____
Telephone	_____	_____	_____	_____
Postal	_____	_____	_____	_____
Dues & publications	_____	_____	_____	_____
Printing & copying	_____	_____	_____	_____
Trash collection	_____	_____	_____	_____
Miscellaneous	_____	_____	_____	_____
Total Expenses	_____	_____	_____	_____
Net Profit (Loss)	_____	_____	_____	_____

Under the heading of *Expenses,* list wages (including any salary you extract from the business), payroll deductions (if you have employees), and all overhead and other expenses associated with operating your business. Add this column, and enter the sum as *Total Expenses.*

Subtract *Total Expenses* from *Gross Income* and enter the result as your projected or estimated *Net Profit (Loss)* for that accounting period.

During your first full year of business, prepare a profit-and-loss report at the end of each quarter. These reports are identical in form to the P&L projections, except that they reflect actual instead of estimated numbers. Comparing the P&L projections with the P&L reports should help you make more precise estimates in the future and more accurate midrange and long-range projections.

Use your first-year P&L projection as your operating budget. At the end of your first full year of operation, use your P&L reports to adjust your projections and create a month-by-month projection and budget for the upcoming year.

In effect, after your first year of business, the second-year projection becomes the first year in your five-year profit-and-loss projection. That is, at the end of each year, you should create a new five-year P&L projection, following the same format as your original P&L projection.

Balance Sheets

A balance sheet is so named because the assets listed in the left column should equal the liabilities in the right column plus the owner's equity. It's a fairly useless document for new businesses and may be of only marginal value for many sole proprietors. (See Chapter 5 for a definition of *sole proprietor.*) Of all the analytical and forecasting documents, I have found the balance sheet the least useful and informative for my home-based business. It might prove useful, however, if you need to seek financing, so you should know what it is and how to create one.

Balance sheets are usually prepared at the end of the year. The so-called *pro forma balance sheet* is one prepared in advance of the coming year or accounting period and is hypothetical in nature.

Balance Sheet

[Your Business Name]

Assets		Liabilities	
Cash (bank accounts)	_____	Accounts Payable	_____
Accounts Receivable	_____	Short-Term Notes	_____
Inventory (if applicable)	_____	Amount Due on Long-Term Notes	_____
Prepaid Expenses	_____	Interest Payable	_____
Short-Term Investments	_____	Taxes Payable	_____
		Payroll	_____
Total Current Assets	$ _____	**Total Current Liabilities**	$ _____
Long-Term Investments	_____		
Land	_____		
Buildings (cost)	_____		
Less Depreciation	_____		
Net Value	$ _____	**Owner's Equity** (assets minus liabilities)	$ _____
Equipment (cost)	_____		
Less Depreciation	_____		
Net Value	$ _____		
Furniture/Fixtures (cost)	_____		
Less Depreciation	_____		
Net Value	$ _____	**Total Liabilities & Equity**	$ _____
Vehicles (cost)	_____		
Less Depreciation	_____		
Net Value	$ _____	Current Date	_____
Total Fixed Assets	$ _____		
Other Assets	$ _____		
Total Assets	$ _____		

Cash-Flow Projections and Reports

Cash flow is more than net profit; it's how money moves into and out of a business. It covers all business income and cash reserves after expenditures and can indicate the timing of cash movement.

For your business to succeed, it's essential that you ensure a steady and substantial income, not only to pay business expenses and to buy materials and equipment, but also to provide you with an adequate personal income and benefits.

You must keep track of cash flow by regular reporting of income and expenditures. In most businesses, this is done monthly, with quarterly and yearly totals included. Accurate and timely records will enable you to track cash flow and forecast future needs and trends, which in turn will allow you to make intelligent capital investments and ward off potential problems or interruptions of cash flow.

Cash-flow projections and reports are similar in form and format to profit-and-loss projections and reports. In fact, they're similar in content, but with two important exceptions. Profit-and-loss projections and reports are designed to provide estimated and actual net profits before taxes, and they do not include cash-reserve information. Cash-flow projections and reports provide estimated and actual after-tax profits plus available cash reserves to indicate a cash position at the end of an accounting period: month, quarter, or year.

To prepare a cash-flow projection for one year, you can use a sheet from a thirteen-column pad or four sheets from a four-column pad as I do. As with the P&L projections and reports, each four-column page provides a column each for three months and one column for quarter totals.

In the left column, Item 1 should be *Cash on Hand* as of the first of the month. This includes any currency earmarked for business purposes as well as amounts in any business bank accounts.

Item 2 is *Cash Receipts* for the month—itemized as cash sales, collected receivables, and any other receipts, including any cash infusion—from your business savings, the sale of capital equipment, or any other source.

Item 3 is *Total Cash Receipts.* Add Item 1 and Item 3 and enter that figure as Item 4: *Total Cash Available.*

Item 5 is *Cash Expenditures.* Under that heading, itemize and list all cash that your business had to pay out during that accounting period, including all wages (yours and any others'), all taxes, all expenses, and all overhead. You can modify this listing to suit your needs. In my own cash-flow projection, I have itemized subheads alphabetically, from *a* to *v*.

Item 6 is *Total Cash Paid:* the sum of everything listed under *Cash Expenditures.* Subtract Item 6 from Item 4 and enter the result as Item 7: *Cash Position.*

At the end of any accounting period, when *Total Cash Available* is greater than *Total Cash Paid,* a positive figure will represent your *Cash Position.* If *Total Cash Paid* is greater than *Total Cash Available,* your *Cash Position* will be a negative figure, also referred to as *negative cash flow.*

The purpose of the cash-flow projection is to identify any negative cash position so that you can take action to rectify the situation.

As with the profit-and-loss documents, you should also prepare a cash-flow report, which is identical to the cash-flow projection except that it reflects actual instead of estimated figures. Regularly comparing the two documents will help you become more accurate in your forecasting.

I know that, barring any unforeseen catastrophe, my most troublesome months will be June and December. They have been for more than ten years and probably will continue to be. For quite a few years, November has been my third most expensive month and May has come up a close fourth.

Not only can I predict which months might slip into a negative cash position, but I also know why. In June and December, in addition to all the usual expenses, I have several hefty semiannual and annual bills to pay—mainly insurance premiums. Also, spring and fall are my busiest seasons, so I'm on the road a good bit then. I always charge my fuel and motel bills to credit cards. This is also a time when I must constantly replenish supplies. It can take from thirty to sixty days for all these charges to show up on my credit-card bills. Those arriving earliest are usually due in May and November, but the bulk of them end up in my accounts-payable file in June and December.

Fifteen years ago I couldn't have made such predictions as I just have. But by preparing certain useful projections and reports and paying attention to how cash moves through my business, I can now do a pretty good job of forecasting trends. Consequently, I'm able to use these figures to my best advantage—whether to tighten my purse strings to see my business through some lean days or make a timely capital investment.

Cash-Flow Projection/Report

(Estimated/Actual)

	January	February	March	First Quarter Totals
1. Cash on Hand (1st of month)	_____	_____	_____	_____
2. Cash Receipts				
a. Cash Sales	_____	_____	_____	_____
b. Collected Receivables	_____	_____	_____	_____
c. Other	_____	_____	_____	_____
3. Total Cash Receipts	_____	_____	_____	_____
4. Total Cash Available	_____	_____	_____	_____
5. Cash Expenditures				
a. Gross Wages	_____	_____	_____	_____
b. Taxes	_____	_____	_____	_____
c. Materials	_____	_____	_____	_____
d. Supplies (office, etc.)	_____	_____	_____	_____
e. Services	_____	_____	_____	_____
f. Repairs & Maintenance	_____	_____	_____	_____
g. Advertising	_____	_____	_____	_____
h. Vehicle	_____	_____	_____	_____
i. Travel & Entertainment	_____	_____	_____	_____
j. Accounting & Legal	_____	_____	_____	_____
k. Rent	_____	_____	_____	_____
l. Telephone	_____	_____	_____	_____
m. Utilities	_____	_____	_____	_____
n. Insurance	_____	_____	_____	_____
o. Printing & Copying	_____	_____	_____	_____
p. Postage	_____	_____	_____	_____
q. UPS, FedEx, etc.	_____	_____	_____	_____
r. Dues & Publications	_____	_____	_____	_____
s. Miscellaneous	_____	_____	_____	_____
t. Other	_____	_____	_____	_____
u. Subtotal	_____	_____	_____	_____
v. Capital Expenditures	_____	_____	_____	_____
6. Total Cash Paid (u plus v)	_____	_____	_____	_____
7. Cash Position (4 minus 6)	_____	_____	_____	_____

Cash-flow analysis can be much more complicated, and usually is, for larger, more complex businesses. Sadly, some writers, consultants, and educators insist the topic be just as cumbersome and confusing for owners of small businesses. They tend to make it an academic exercise that serves little practical purpose for the home-based entrepreneur. My advice is this: Try to keep it as simple as possible.

Credit and Borrowing

Although many entrepreneurs start businesses on borrowed capital, I don't recommend this practice. Instead of borrowing start-up cash, you stand a much better chance of succeeding if you work part time, invest in equipment, and build a substantial savings account before launching a full-time business. Don't start with long-term debt.

Credit Cards and Vendor Accounts

Short-term debt is another matter, and it takes many shapes. Every time you pay for a tank of gas with an oil-company credit card, you aren't really paying for it; you're putting off payment until the company sends you a bill. Likewise with the motel bill you put on an American Express card, the computer software you charge to a Visa account, or the tool purchase you put on a MasterCard. When you charge office and craft supplies and materials to accounts you have established with vendors, you also take on short-term debt.

This form of borrowing is not only an acceptable practice, but it also can offer a number of advantages when properly managed. Credit cards and vendor accounts can be a great aid to bookkeeping. They eliminate the need to keep large amounts of cash on hand and they reduce the number of checks you must write.

They also speed up delivery of mail orders because your supplier can ship immediately instead of waiting for a check to clear. If you run into a problem with a supplier, you stand a better chance of getting quick satisfaction if you charged your order to a major credit card, because the credit-card company will contact the supplier on your behalf. This not only saves you time and trouble, but it also exerts more pressure on the supplier than you could ever hope to.

If you can avoid the expensive trap of revolving credit and pay all your credit-card and other accounts in full as the bills arrive, you will soon build a good credit rating that will serve you well if you need to seek long-term financing.

Credit-Card Traps

Along with the notoriously and unnecessarily high interest rates that many credit-card issuers charge are other costs you should be aware of and should try to avoid. Some of the features and services that credit-card companies offer might sound great but prove to be only marginally valuable or utterly useless. Moreover, some companies use ploys to attract potential cardholders by playing on their egos.

Whenever you consider signing up for a credit card, look for a company that charges little or nothing in the way of annual fees. If any annual fee exceeds $25, go elsewhere, or make sure the company offers useful features and incentives that make such a fee worth paying.

At one time, major credit-card companies charged no annual fee and no interest on new purchases for about the first thirty days. Instead, they made their profits from the interest they charged on revolving credit. Now many companies not only are charging annual fees but also have eliminated the grace period on new purchases, thus earning interest on all purchases from the moment they're charged to the account. Try to find companies that allow a grace period of twenty-five to thirty days on all new purchases; then pay off your accounts as they come due. This way you will be able to make interest-free credit purchases and build an outstanding credit record in the process.

Some credit-card companies that charge exorbitant annual fees and high interest rates try to attract business by offering cardholders incentives, ranging from discounts on car rentals and lodging to travel-club benefits and annual financial reports. Make sure that any such features will be of real value to you and your business.

Several of my credit cards and memberships in professional associations entitle me to 10 percent discounts on car rentals at specific agencies. These discounts, however, are usually disallowed on special low-cost rental packages. By shopping around for the best deal, I have always beaten the paltry 10 percent discount—a worthless feature for me that probably will be for you as well.

I travel a good bit, so when a company offered me its highly touted Corporate Card, with discounts of 20 to 50 percent on hotel rooms, I jumped at the chance. I thought I could save a bundle, so the $75 annual fee didn't bother me. What I later learned, however, was that few of the hotel chains on the small list of cooperating establishments had facilities in the cities I visit. I canceled the card before paying the annual fee.

I also canceled one Gold Card when it became obvious that I was paying $75 a year simply for the color gold. None of the other card privileges was of any value to me. A colleague of mine canceled his $300-a-year Platinum Card for similar reasons.

Credit-card marketing people will try to inflate your ego by telling you how important you'll be when you carry their gold or platinum card. In reality, however, nobody gives a hoot about the color of your card. As long as accounts are in good standing and charges have not exceeded credit limits, in vendors' eyes, all cards are the color of greenbacks.

Debit Cards

Many banks issue debit cards, which resemble credit cards only in appearance. As with many credit cards, purchases made by debit card are usually charged to the user's account immediately. Furthermore, some banks charge a transaction fee every time the debit card is used.

Worse yet, while the maximum liability to the cardholder for unauthorized use of a lost or stolen credit card is $50, liability for the holder of a debit card can be as much as $500.

My advice is simple: User beware, and read the fine print in the debit-card agreement before signing.

Long-Term Debt

Even if you adopt a policy of avoiding long-term debt, sooner or later you will probably have to borrow for your business. For example, you may have to replace an expensive piece of equipment, upgrade a computer system, or buy a new vehicle. It's not always possible to make such high-ticket purchases without a long-term loan.

You might also land contracts that force you to borrow for capital investment. For example, doing the best and most cost-effective job might hinge on your owning certain equipment. Or it could be that just as you are trying to get a few more months' use out of your vehicle, your business suddenly begins demanding considerable travel. These are times when borrowing now could pay off handsomely later.

Under such circumstances, be sure to shop around for the best interest rates. Before you visit bankers, head for your local Small Business Development Center (SBDC) or write to the U.S. Small Business Administration (SBA) for information about its loan programs, such as the guaranteed-loan program, export revolving line of credit, and small-loan program. The SBDC can alert you to any other state and federal programs for which you might qualify. Among the most common are special loans for veterans, women, and members of minority groups.

Know What's on Your Credit Report

Everybody in America who has a credit history is in the computer files of at least one credit-reporting company. It can cost $25 or more to obtain a single report on anyone, including yourself, from one of these companies, but you are entitled to one copy of your own credit report free of charge, except for a small handling fee. Your bank should be able to handle the transaction, and I recommend you make this a top priority.

Many people have complained about errors in their credit reports, which have caused them trouble when applying for loans. You need to examine your own credit report to determine your credit rating and the accuracy of the information in the report. If you find errors, get them corrected immediately; they can affect your credit rating and interfere with your ability to secure financing.

Chapter Four
Financial Management

O ne of the most important and difficult questions that faces every aspiring home-based entrepreneur is, "How much should I charge for my products or services?" I have no pat answers or useful formulas to help you with this question because there are too many variables to consider. I can no more tell you what to charge your customers than a bed-and-breakfast innkeeper in Fargo can tell a San Diego hotel owner how to set rates. Both might be in the lodging business, but beyond that, there are simply too many differences.

Local cost of living is a major determinant. It's far cheaper to live and do business in North Dakota than in California. Even one part of a state can differ greatly from another. In northern California, for example, you can still find a clean, comfortable, modern motel room for less than $50 a night; in southern California, I've seen RV spaces go for that much.

Every business is different. One artisan might specialize in beadwork while another works exclusively as a potter. In a more diversified business, one individual may make and sell toys, puzzles, games, and a variety of country crafts. Some peddle their wares directly to local gift and specialty shops, whereas others prefer to handle only the creative side of the business and let a representative or agent take care of sales. An artisan in New York, Los Angeles, or Seattle may have to gross $600 a day to make a living; one based in rural mid-America might get by on $300 a day in sales and live just as comfortably.

Only you can determine what to charge for your craft products and talents, so you will have to do your homework. Although some books and associations can help, in the end your pricing policy will be based on what crafts you produce, how you operate, how you stack up against the competition, where you sell your work, and where you do your work.

No matter what craft constitutes your main business interest, you'll have your work cut out for you in the initial pricing process. You will also find that you must constantly monitor costs and competition so that you will know when and how much to increase prices.

Don't fret. Expect some difficulty in the beginning, and be assured that you'll learn from trial and error. You'll probably make some mistakes, as most of us do. You'll know you've overpriced some items when they don't sell well. And you'll kick yourself when a new product line sells out immediately because you've underpriced it. Take comfort in the fact that pricing and price monitoring become much easier with time.

As in any craft business, your prices will depend mainly on the cost of running your business (overhead), the cost of materials, the value of your time, and the pricing structure of the marketplace (what the market will bear).

Pricing for Profit

Before establishing prices, you will have to determine what kinds of crafts you will be creating and selling, then research those areas to determine how payment is commonly made and what it amounts to. If you plan to operate a ceramics studio, find out what other ceramists in your community or region are charging. This will provide a basis for your pricing structure—a figure to work with. Then determine how you fit into the community of local or regional ceramists.

You don't want to start out as the most expensive ceramist in town; nor should you be the cheapest. If your products are top quality and your pricing is midrange, you can gradually increase prices as your reputation for quality and reliability grows. Even if you can work considerably cheaper than other artisans in your locale, undercutting their prices could work against you in several ways. First, your low prices will turn away some potential customers who reason that you get what you pay for. What's more, they might invite your competitors to retaliate.

In my diversified business, income derives from many sources, including royalties, day rates, hourly jobs, flat fees, and consignments as well as wholesale and retail sales. Obviously, I've had to spend considerable time analyzing my costs and factoring in my labor and profit margins to know what I need to make. Then I've had to make adjustments according to market trends and pressures. You'll have to do the same.

Direct Costs

The direct costs associated with the manufacture of any craft include money spent for raw materials and finishing products as well as for any directly related services.

For example, a clock maker who makes wall clocks from maple burl slabs might cut his own slabs from raw burls, have them cut at a mill, or buy ready-cut slabs. If he buys the burls and cuts them himself, what he pays for the burls is a direct material cost. The work he does to cut and prepare the burls is labor, which is another, albeit important, part of the equation.

If the clock maker buys the burls and has them cut into slabs at a mill, the burls are a direct material cost, to which the mill charges can be added as a direct expense.

If he buys ready-cut burls, they are considered raw material, and what he pays is considered a direct cost.

Prices charged for clockworks, hanging hardware, and polyurethane varnish are also direct material costs. If he has a local wood shop finish-sand the slabs and an artist paint scenes on the sanded slabs, those are direct expenses.

All these direct costs constitute one part of the formula for determining what to charge for the finished clocks. What the clock maker pays to heat and light his shop, however, are indirect costs, which are treated separately in arriving at the total cost of manufacture.

Overhead

In determining what it costs to manufacture any item, you also must include the indirect costs, known as overhead. These costs include rent, utilities, office supplies, depreciation, and anything else that's not a direct material or labor cost. Most of the methods of calculating overhead when pricing a product are complicated and time consuming and are of marginal value for most home-based craft professionals.

One fairly simple way to factor overhead into the pricing scheme is to determine indirect costs, then calculate an hourly rate for them. This method works fine for service-oriented businesses, where hourly rates tend to be high, but not so well for product-oriented craft businesses.

The only sure way to determine per-item overhead is to do careful time-and-cost studies that, in a small business, simply devour too much valuable time for what they're worth.

Most of us resort to formulas that aren't much better than guesses but take far less time and work out all right in the end.

In one formula we're advised to consider indirect costs to be the equivalent of one-third of the direct costs. In other words, Direct Costs x 33.3% = Overhead.

A variation on the one-third theme suggests treating overhead as equivalent to one-third the cost of materials or one-third the cost of labor, whichever is greater.

Ya pays your money, ya takes your pick.

Labor

You must factor all labor, including your own, into the pricing equation. Labor is worth money, and it is one of the costs of manufacture.

If you're doing all the work, include your labor as part of the price of any craft object, but avoid the temptation of overpricing your labor. As the owner/manager of a successful business, perhaps your time is worth $30, $40, or more an hour, but you can't consider time spent cutting, assembling, and finishing parts of a craft object to be worth that much. When you're managing, you're worth a manager's salary; when you're laboring, you should collect a laborer's wages.

To determine how much value to assign to labor, simply find out what it would cost in your locale to hire others to perform identical or similar tasks. If you could hire someone for $10 an hour, consider your labor worth $10 an hour when you do the same job.

Profit

Profit is another important part of the pricing equation, but oddly enough, it's something too many artisans ignore or confuse with labor costs. Profit and labor costs are not the same. As regards product pricing, labor—including *your* labor—is part of the cost of manufacturing the product. Profit is the company's share: what's left after all other costs.

Profit is what will allow you to expand your business, to invest in it. It's the money that will make you more money. It's the reward for your managing skills. It's the payback for the risks you take, for the extra hours you put in, for the initiative you show, for the responsibility you dare not shirk. It's what operating your own business is all about.

A friend of mine is a craftsman, and a good one. His major problem is that he doesn't consider his time very valuable. He says he has to make $100 a day to survive. If he meant $100 in profit, over and above his cost of manufacturing, that would be okay. If he were talking about $100 a day for labor, in addition to whatever profit he might make, that might be all right too. But he means he's satisfied making $100 total, after the cost of materials and overhead, and he doesn't have a good grasp of what his overhead amounts to. Twenty to thirty years ago, his $100 a day would have been good money, but not today.

In my business, I say that to spend a dollar I have to make two. When the year-end tallies are in, it usually ends up that way. Some years it's a little better, some years a little worse. Certain aspects of my business are better, or more profitable, than others.

What my friend fails to realize when he looks at that $100, literally or figuratively, at the end of a workday, is that he's not really looking at $100. By the time all the federal, state, and county taxing agencies finish with him, 40 percent of that $100 will be gone. Another 10 percent will just disappear incidentally, leaving him with about $50 to show for his day's efforts. For his usual ten-hour day, his take-home pay is about five bucks an hour, and there's no additional profit to plow back into the business. Fifty hours a week, fifty weeks a year—after expenses, taxes, and incidentals—works out to $12,500. And he wonders why he just can't seem to get ahead.

Again, profit is in addition to, over and above, above and beyond, everything else. If your business isn't making a profit, your business isn't succeeding.

So how do you determine what your profit should be? It's easy—just a loose translation of the old Golden Rule: Do to others as others do to you. If you sell craft items to gift shops for resale, to arrive at their selling prices, the shop owners simply double your price, or mark up 100 percent. If you sell an item for $10, the shop sells it for $20, or probably $19.95. If you sell an item for $100, its new price tag will probably read $199.95.

Figure your business's profit the same way. Add all the costs of manufacture and multiply that times 100 percent to determine your profit. Then add profit to the equation to arrive at the price.

Pricing Equation

Here's the simple pricing equation:

$$\text{Materials} + \text{Overhead} + \text{Labor} + \text{Profit} = \text{Price}$$

It's easy to arrive at a price for any item, providing you have kept good records. Let's assume you're making a product that takes two hours per unit and that labor costs are $10 an hour. We'll further assume that your materials and any directly related services amount to $8.50 per unit. With that small amount of information, and using the second variation of the one-third formula for calculating overhead, make the following list and calculations to determine the price to charge for each unit:

- Labor = $10/hour
- Time per unit = 2 hours = $20.00
- Materials per unit = $8.50
- Overhead = $20 x 33.3% = $6.66
- Cost of manufacture = $35.16
- Profit = $35.16 x 100% = $35.16
- Price per unit = $70.32 (wholesale)

If you're selling this product wholesale for $70, the retailer will mark up 100 percent and charge his customers $139.95. This equation works as well for a $10 item as for a $1,000 item.

Psychological Pricing Schemes

Any observant buyer knows there are a number of pricing schemes in use that fool some buyers into believing they're getting more for their money or are paying less than they actually are.

"Twofers" are popular in supermarkets and some discount stores. A canned product, for example, will sell better when marked two for a dollar than when marked 50 cents or even 49 cents each. Any item will sell much better priced at $1.99 or $4.98 than at $2.00 or $5.00, respectively.

At craft fairs, flea markets, swap meets, and other public sales, you might find it a nuisance to fool with pennies. So price your $10 items at $9.95, $20 items at $19.95, and $50 items at $49.95.

You can eliminate the pennies, nickels, and dimes and carry only paper money and a couple of rolls of quarters by pricing amounts under a dollar in twenty-five-cent denominations: $9.75, $18.75, $22.50, $49.50, and so on.

Reducing Costs to Increase Profits

The cost of everything that goes into your craft products—materials, supplies, overhead, and labor—affects profit. Your costs must be factored into the prices you charge your customers. Excessive costs can make your prices too high to compete effectively. One result is that you could price yourself out of business.

Consequently, you must remain ever alert for ways to reduce costs and thereby keep your profits up. You also must track your costs to know how to accommodate them in your pricing structure. Macro cost analysis is a continuing process in any well-run business, and the best tools for this job are your profit-and-loss projections and reports.

Micro cost analysis is equally important, and for this you will need to keep accurate cost-and-time studies on every product in your line. It's also a good idea to review your products regularly to look for ways of reducing costs, thereby increasing profits. You'll need to study your manufacturing processes as well as your time-and-cost records to see if there are ways you can make profitable improvements.

Managing Accounts Payable

Bills that come due regularly or irregularly are known as accounts payable. There's more to managing this crucial part of your business than simply writing checks and mailing them. You should do so in a timely fashion, and you must understand the difference between timely and on time.

If you merely stack up all your bills and write checks until you have no more money, you aren't managing well. Although most of your bills are probably payable in thirty days, some vendors offer discounts for payment early in the month—usually something in the range of 1 to 5 percent if paid by the tenth of the month, then net after that. Some vendors make their bills payable in thirty days with no discount option. A typical monthly statement might show "Terms: 2% 10 days—Net 30." That means you have ten days from the date of the statement to deduct 2 percent from your bill; after that you must pay the full amount and must do so within one month.

Some suppliers don't send monthly statements but instead expect you to pay off the invoice. You might be allowed a total of thirty days to pay, or until the thirtieth of the month following the invoice date. If the supplier offers an early-payment discount, the invoice might say something like "Terms: 3% 10th proximo—net 30th," which means you may take a 3 percent discount if you pay by the tenth of the month following the invoice date.

Timely Payments

If your checking account is fat, you can just pay all your bills at one sitting, but for most of us, checks and bills arrive throughout the month. Often a checking account balance might make it through only a portion of the bills and need to await the arrival and deposit of the next batch of receivables.

In such circumstances, sort all your bills into stacks, including those offering discounts for early payment, those offering no discounts, and those offering no discounts and charging late-payment penalties. Obviously, the bills to pay first are the discounted ones. I have several vendors who offer 10 percent discounts and one that offers 20 percent; they get paid first every month. Next, pay those that will penalize you for late payment. That way, if you have a slight interruption of cash flow toward the end of the month, you won't have to miss paying a bill that carries a penalty with it.

When the Buck Stops Short

If you continually come up short at the end of the month, you must make some adjustments in your cash-management practices. You should strive to get all your bills paid on time and in a timely way, but when the buck stops short, you need to take action.

Occasionally letting an outstanding balance slip into the thirty-day past-due category is no big deal and will have little or no effect on your credit rating. Balances that go to sixty days are more serious, and ninety days will have your creditors worrying about you.

If you run into a cash-flow problem, the first thing to do is to try to inject cash into your business to rectify it. If that's impossible, or if it might cause more serious problems elsewhere, don't just ignore your bills.

Immediately write to your creditors to explain the circumstances, assure them that this is a temporary situation that you will correct soon, and provide a date they can count on for full payment.

I ended up in such a position several years ago after I had placed large orders for materials and office supplies, counting on a substantial check due to be sent to me. When the check didn't arrive as promised, several of my payables were put in jeopardy.

I had charged the materials to a credit card, so I made the minimum payment due and let the balance slip into the high-interest revolving-credit category. I had charged the office supplies to my account with the vendor, to whom I wrote a letter and assured full payment within forty-five days. Three weeks later, the tardy check arrived, and I paid my bill and added a 2 percent late charge. Two weeks later I got a letter from the vendor thanking me for the payment and a check refunding the late charge.

Such timely and professional action will leave your credit rating intact and might even improve it. Show your business associates that you're a reliable professional, and you'll be treated like one.

Managing Accounts Receivable

Everything owed to you falls into the category of *accounts receivable,* often just called *receivables.* Managing receivables is one of the most important aspects of controlling your business's finances.

Get the Cash When You Can

Cash is always best; take it when you can get it. It's impossible, however, to run a craft business without getting involved in credit in one way or another. Whenever you agree to sell your products and get paid later, you are extending credit. That means credit management is a crucial part of your business.

Billing Practices

Your first step toward managing receivables is to establish systematic billing practices. For most of us, that means stocking and using invoice forms and monthly statement forms. You can pick the forms that best suit your business and have them imprinted with your name, address, and phone number. An alternative is to use a computer to design and generate your own forms. Most word-processing software will facilitate form printing, or you can use any of a number of small-business and form-making programs. Some companies offer multipart, preprinted forms and dedicated software to streamline the billing process.

You must adopt a billing policy and use it consistently. You can use invoices and monthly statements or invoices alone. In the latter case, ask your clients or customers to pay the invoice and include instructions to that effect on the invoice: *This is the only bill you will receive. Please pay the amount due.*

I use invoices and statements because the statement often serves as a low-key, impersonal dun on accounts that slip into the thirty-days-past category. So I bill each sale with an invoice; then at month's end I send a statement to each customer with an outstanding balance. I spell out all details of the transaction on the invoice. On the subsequent statement I need only reference each unpaid invoice by number and show the amount due.

Late Charges and Follow-Up

This important message appears at the bottom of every invoice and statement: *2% per month (24% APR) applied to the balance of all accounts after 30 days.* Accounts that go past thirty days get a 2 percent charge added to the balance. After sixty days I also use a bold, red *Past Due* stamp on the statement.

Every account ninety days past due gets the same treatment as the sixty-day account, plus a letter from me insisting on immediate payment. If the account goes to 120 days, I send a demand letter by certified mail, insisting on payment within ten days. The next step is a phone call to my attorney for a ten-day demand letter on his letterhead.

INVOICE

Arts & Crafts Unlimited

1492 Columbus Drive

Moon Valley, IN 54321

Phone: (123) 555–4545 • Fax: (123) 555–6767

Bill to: Ship to:

_____   _____

_____   _____

_____   _____

_____   _____

Invoice #_____   Date_____   Customer Order #_____

Terms _____

Quantity	Item/Description	Price	Amount

Total Amount Due:

2% per month (24% APR) applied to the balance of all accounts after 30 days

INVOICE

Arts & Crafts Unlimited
1492 Columbus Drive
Moon Valley, IN 54321
Phone: (123) 555–4545 • Fax: (123) 555–6767

Bill to:

Woodwright's Gift Shop

P.O. Box 4231

Cincinnati, OH 45210

Ship to:

Bill Baily, Manager

Woodwright's Gift Shop

1760 Old Stage Road

Cincinnati, OH 45212

Invoice # 1-011503-4   Date Jan 15, 2003   Customer Order # _____

Terms _____ Net 30 days _____

Quantity	Item/Description	Price	Amount
10	Alder Mug Trees	$ 14.50	$145.00
5	Oak Cutlery Racks	12.20	61.00
2	Myrtlewood Clocks	65.00	130.00
10	Maple-Burl Plaques	12.25	122.50
1	Rosewood Tray	75.00	75.00
1	Laminated Jewelry Box	125.00	125.00
	TOTAL MERCHANDISE		$658.50
	SHIPPING AND HANDLING		65.85

Total Amount Due: $724.35

2% per month (24% APR) applied to the balance of all accounts after 30 days

STATEMENT

Arts & Crafts Unlimited

1492 Columbus Drive
Moon Valley, IN 54321
Phone: (123) 555–4545 • Fax: (123) 555–6767

To:

_____   Date _____

_____   Terms _____

_____   Account Number _____

_____   Amount Past Due _____

Date	Invoice Number/Description	Charges	Credits	Balance
	BALANCE FORWARD →			

Pay Last Amount
In This Column

2% per month (24% APR) applied to the balance of all accounts after 30 days

STATEMENT

Arts & Crafts Unlimited
1492 Columbus Drive
Moon Valley, IN 54321
Phone: (123) 555–4545 • Fax: (123) 555–6767

To:

Accounts Payable

Woodwright's Gift Shop

P.O. Box 4231

Cincinnati, OH 45210

Date _January 31, 2003_

Terms _Net 30 days_

Account Number _00123_

Amount Past Due _____

Date	Invoice Number/Description	Charges	Credits	Balance
	BALANCE FORWARD →			$226.60
1-2-03	Invoice #1-010203-2	$291.50		518.10
1-10-03	PAYMENT - Thank You!		$226.60	291.50
1-15-03	Invoice #1-011503-4	724.35		$1,015.85

Pay Last Amount
In This Column

2% per month (24% APR) applied to the balance of all accounts after 30 days

The lawyer's demand letter works nearly every time, but that one letter costs me $50, so I don't use it for small amounts.

If all those measures fail, I'm faced with the decision to turn the account over to a collection agency or to sue. I have faced such circumstances only twice. In one instance, I decided the likelihood of collection was slim, and the amount wasn't worth the time and trouble, so I wrote it off. In the other case the amount was worth going after, but even though I was skeptical about the client's promise to pay, I agreed to let her postpone payment for six more months. Three months later her attorney sent me notice of bankruptcy and invited me to stop by to pick up my check for a penny on the dollar, which wouldn't have paid fuel expenses for the round-trip. There's a lesson in there somewhere for all of us.

Purchasing

Purchasing is an ongoing process in any business. You will need to spend money on office supplies, craft supplies and materials, furniture and fixtures, office equipment, craft equipment, and tools.

It won't take long for you to get a feel for stocking office and craft supplies and materials and to know what items you need to keep on hand. You'll want to place orders regularly but will probably find monthly to be too frequent. I try to order quarterly because that keeps paperwork to a minimum and enables me to buy in money-saving quantities. Sometimes I buy more than a three-month supply to take advantage of sales.

Ask for Discounts

Unless you are already buying at rock-bottom prices, don't hesitate to ask your suppliers for better prices, especially local vendors, and particularly if you buy in quantity. For example, you shouldn't have to pay a local craft supplier the same prices that the casual walk-in does. You represent volume buying and repeat business. If the proprietor doesn't understand this, find another supplier.

Buying Office Supplies

When I started my business, I bought all my office supplies locally, but local vendors' prices eventually drove me out of town. Now I buy all office supplies by phone or on-line and save an astounding amount of money each year.

When my printer introduced me to Quill Corporation and gave me one of the company's catalogs, I started comparing prices and was shocked. The four-column pads I was buying locally for $3.88 each were available from Quill for 89 cents apiece in quantities of ten or more. File-folder labels that cost $4.71 a package locally were $1.29 at Quill. Vinyl binders that sold locally for $4.00 to $11.00 were in the Quill catalog for 89 cents apiece in quantity.

I could buy retail from Quill, add a 200 percent markup, and still sell office supplies for less than the local stationers do. By the way, Quill has toll-free phone and fax numbers, pays the shipping on all orders more than $45, seldom back-orders anything, and delivers to my doorstep, usually the next day. (You'll find the Quill address in the "Source Directory" at the back of this book, under "Direct Sales Outlets: Business and Office Equipment and Supplies.")

Buying Craft Supplies

Unless you live in a small town or rural area or use highly specialized craft tools and materials, you should be able to shop locally for many of your craft supplies. You need to shop wisely to keep your production costs down and your prices competitive. If local prices are too high and nearby dealers are unwilling to offer sufficient discounts, you have no choice but to go elsewhere for your craft supplies. And you will certainly have to shop out of town if you can't find what you need locally.

Two books you should add to your reference shelf will lead you to hundreds of sources for craft tools and materials. Order them from your favorite bookstore, or find them on-line at amazon.com or barnesandnoble.com.

The Catalog of Catalogs VI by Edward L. Palder is a fat volume of 570 pages, listing 15,000 catalogs in more than 900 subject areas. In its well-organized pages, you'll find names, addresses, phone numbers, fax lines, and Web sites for all kinds of tools and mate-

PURCHASE ORDER

Arts & Crafts Unlimited

1492 Columbus Drive

Moon Valley, IN 54321

Phone: (123) 555–4545 • Fax: (123) 555–6767

To:

_____   Date _____

_____   Purchase Order # _____

_____   Customer Account #_____

_____   Ship Via _____

	Quantity	Item Number	Item Description	Price	Amount
1					
2					
3					
4					
5					
6					
7					
8					
9					
10					
11					
12					
13					
14					
15					
16					
17					

PLEASE INCLUDE ONE COPY OF YOUR INVOICE WITH THE SHIPMENT OF THIS ORDER

PURCHASE ORDER

Arts & Crafts Unlimited

1492 Columbus Drive

Moon Valley, IN 54321

Phone: (123) 555–4545 • Fax: (123) 555–6767

To:

Crafty Woody's Woodcraft Supply

4440 Winchester Drive

Chicago, IL 60606

Date _January 11, 2003_

Purchase Order # _P-011103_

Customer Account # _4321-0001-6541-9876_ _Expires 9/06_

Ship Via _UPS Ground_

	Quantity	Item Number	Item Description	Price	Amount
1	20 packs	94912	Oak Shaker Pegs	$ 3.85	$ 77.00
2	20 packs	65912	Walnut Shaker Pegs	4.45	89.00
3	20 packs	10348	Birch Mug-Tree Pegs	3.15	63.00
4	20 packs	33738	Oak Mug-Tree Pegs	3.95	79.00
5	10	15032	Oak Gallery Rails	14.95	149.50
6	10 pairs	96032	Oak Corner Posts	3.75	37.50
7	10 packs	24307	1/4" Fluted Dowel Pins	1.15	11.50
8	10 packs	76307	3/8" Fluted Dowel Pins	1.50	15.00
9	1 gallon	77107	Titebond II Glue	19.95	19.95
10					
11			TOTAL MERCHANDISE		$541.45
12			SHIPPING & HANDLING		16.24
13			TOTAL ORDER		$557.69
14					
15					
16					
17					

PLEASE INCLUDE ONE COPY OF YOUR INVOICE WITH THE SHIPMENT OF THIS ORDER rials. A *Popular Mechanics* review of the book said, *"The Catalog of Catalogs* is a reference designed to help you spend less time looking for stuff and more time doing—whatever it may be. Its thickness only hints at the wide variety of sources you'll find in it."

The other volume—more specialized, but right up our alley—is *Crafts Supply Source Book* by Margaret A. Boyd. This is another conveniently organized book and a must for every serious craft enthusiast. It provides 2,000 annotated listings in fifty-eight categories, complete with addresses and essential numbers, as well as e-mail and Web site information.

Numbering Systems

Preprinted invoice and purchase-order forms come unnumbered or sequentially numbered. If you use unnumbered forms or forms you design yourself, you'll have to devise a numbering system. You can use a simple sequential numbering system, but you'll need to have a way to keep track of the last invoice or purchase order you sent, which can be troublesome. Whatever system you use or invent, make sure that you never duplicate a number. That way, each invoice and purchase order is specific and unique.

Some people prefer a numbering system that employs a six-digit date. It's easy to track, prevents duplication, and is easily modified to fit any situation. To distinguish invoice numbers from purchase-order numbers, prefix the invoice numbers with the letter *I* and purchase orders with the letter *P*. If you're sending more than one invoice or purchase order on any day, add a sequentially numbered suffix to each.

Had I used such a system when sending out a batch of invoices on February 16, 2003, here's how it would have worked: The six-digit date was 021603. The first invoice in the batch would have been numbered I–021603–1, the second I–021603–2, and so on. If I had sent but one purchase order that day, its number would have been P–021603.

This system is foolproof and couldn't be simpler.

Is the Lowest Price Always the Best Price?

If you can get the lowest prices and great service, as I do with Quill Corporation, that's the best of both worlds, but it rarely works out that way. You often have to sacrifice one for the other. But when it's a close call, give your business to a local company.

For the first two years I was in business in Oregon, I gave a considerable amount of business to a local shop. I never got a nickel off anything I ever bought there, and when I asked the owner about a professional discount, all I got was a vacant stare.

A friend and local high-school teacher recommended another shop he was dealing with. I no sooner introduced myself to the owner than he offered me a flat 20 percent discount on everything but sale items. Because his prices are generally higher than those at mail-order suppliers, I don't buy high-ticket items from him, but his prices on most materials and supplies end up being only slightly higher than my mail-order sources.

It's no more difficult to buy supplies by mail, and I would save a little by doing so. Nevertheless, I buy most of my supplies from my local dealer, and with good reason. When I need special services and I'm on a tight deadline, my local supplier is there for me as no distant mail-order supplier would be. He even opened his shop for me on a Sunday when I had an emergency and was faced with a Monday shipping deadline. Failure to meet that deadline could have cost me dearly in future business lost.

Sometimes the lowest price isn't the best price.

Fiscal Conservatism

If new business operators have a common fault, it's their overly optimistic view of how their businesses will fare. For that reason, it's best to adopt a conservative outlook and tight-fisted management policy.

Don't go into business thinking you'll get rich. Plan instead to work hard for an adequate living. If you eventually get rich, good for you. Won't it be a pleasant surprise?

Chapter Five
The Legal Aspects of Your Craft Business

L egal affairs, like filing, are necessary nuisances in every business. Although your craft business isn't likely to become entangled in all the legal debris many businesses must contend with these days, there are legal matters you must consider. The first is to determine how your business should be legally structured.

Sole Proprietorship

Most of us who work out of our homes are classified as sole proprietors. That is, we are the only principals involved in the ownership and management of our businesses, and we are the only ones responsible for the outcome. We *solely* reap the benefits, pay the bills, and suffer the consequences of liability.

Even if you now have or eventually will have other people working for or with you, you will probably remain the sole proprietor of your business. Having someone else working in your business in no way changes its status. As sole proprietor, you will be the owner and manager of your business, which has certain advantages and disadvantages.

Advantages of Sole Proprietorship

On the plus side is simplicity. There's not much to setting up a sole proprietorship. You aren't encumbered with endless paperwork, and you don't need a lawyer to advise you or create documents for the operation of your business. You pay taxes via your personal return—Schedule C of Form 1040—and your tax rates will usually be lower than corporate rates.

Disadvantages of Sole Proprietorship

Among the disadvantages of sole proprietorship is difficulty in obtaining outside financing, especially during the start-up stage. You will be entirely responsible for any legal and financial problems your business encounters. You will probably pay much more for health insurance than other, larger businesses do, and you will be able to deduct only that portion of your premiums allowed on Schedule A (Itemized Deductions) of Form 1040.

The vast majority of home-based entrepreneurs are sole proprietors. Be aware, however, that you're not bound to that status forever. But even if you eventually find partnership or incorporation advantageous, you will probably want to start out as a sole proprietor.

Partnership

When two or more persons go into business together, they usually form some sort of partnership. Partners share profits, expenses, responsibilities, and liabilities. They might own equal divisions of the business or have some other limited arrangement.

Partners enjoy the same tax breaks as sole proprietors. Each reports business profit and loss on Schedule C of Form 1040. It's fairly easy to set up a partnership and doesn't cost much in the way of attorney's fees.

Advantages of Partnership

Among the advantages of partnership for home-based businesses is the division of major equipment costs. For example, partners who work in the same crafts can share the costs of such major capital investments as stationary power tools, kilns, looms, and such, then work out agreeable schedules for the use of the equipment.

Sharing costs and the use of many high-ticket items makes sense because such equipment often stands idle much of the time. Partners can share computer hardware and software, expensive copying and duplicating equipment, and storage facilities.

The sharing of labor and brainpower can lead to lucrative and enjoyable ventures. Travel to and setup at craft fairs and other exhibits are much easier when there are partners to share the work.

Disadvantages of Partnership

Partnerships face the same financial difficulties and liabilities as sole proprietorships. Division of management responsibilities can lead to disagreements. And there are always potential problems when a partner leaves the business for whatever reason.

Persons considering partnership must breach numerous obstacles and work out many potential problems. Will the business operate out of one home or both? If one, which one? Will the partners carry equal workloads? How will they measure work? Will investments be equal?

Partnership Agreement

Any partnership requires a good written agreement. The better and more complete the agreement, the fewer the hassles down the line. Partners should spend time, individually and together, considering, discussing, and writing down everything pertaining to the business and partnership. Set everything you can think of in writing.

Give an attorney a copy of the document you and your partner or partners have created and set up a later meeting date. Your attorney should then draft an agreement for approval by all parties. After corrections, additions, and deletions, the attorney will draft the final agreement for the partners' signatures.

The agreement should make provisions for division of expenditures, profits, losses, responsibilities, and liabilities as well as prolonged illness, disability, or death of a partner. You must also consider the disposition of the share of a partner who retires from the business or leaves for any other reason. Include a buyout clause, and have your attorney advise you on restrictions pertaining to buying and selling of the business or any partner's share. You may want to include nondisclosure and noncompetition clauses.

The agreement can be revised or amended at any time and should be whenever the partners make major changes in the way the business is operated. Put it in writing, and keep it current.

Limited-Liability Company

A limited-liability company is similar to a partnership but enjoys some of the advantages usually restricted to corporations. If you're thinking about forming a partnership, ask your attorney about the possibility and advantages of forming a limited-liability company.

Corporation

It's highly unlikely that you will want to consider incorporating when you start your business; in fact, you may never wish to incorporate. In the event your circumstances change, however, you should know something about the pros and cons. A good attorney and accountant will be able to advise you on this major step.

Incorporation can be expensive. You will certainly need an attorney's help, and you will have to pay your state a fee that might amount to $1,000 or more.

In a sole proprietorship or partnership, the principals are the business, and vice versa; everything that affects the business affects the owners. A corporation is an entity in and of itself.

Advantages of Incorporation

In a corporation, shareholders' assets are protected, and corporate assets are initially protected by current bankruptcy laws. Depending on the type of business, corporations generally find financing more readily available than sole proprietorships and partnerships do.

Disadvantages of Incorporation

On the downside, corporations are much more complicated and expensive to set up. Most pay high corporate tax rates. In general, a corporation faces more complications, with requirements for bylaws, a board of directors, corporate officers, annual meetings, and greater need for attorneys and accountants.

Zoning Ordinances

Municipalities and counties throughout the nation create urban and rural zones to allow, prohibit, promote, or discourage various activities. Certain areas and neighborhoods might be zoned agricultural, industrial, light industrial, heavy industrial, commercial, residential, or even such combinations as multiresidential or commercial-residential.

In some residential neighborhoods all business is prohibited, no matter what form it takes. Such restrictive zoning, however, is rare.

Obviously, you'll have no problem running your business in any industrial, commercial, or commercial-residential zone. Nor will county officials give you any trouble about operating in an agricultural zone.

Restrictive zoning of most residential neighborhoods is aimed at businesses that create noise, pollution, heavy traffic, and other activities best confined to industrial and commercial zones. Many allow professional and service businesses to operate, as well as any clean and quiet craft business, so you probably won't have any opposition to your running a home-based craft business. You need to be sure, though, so you'll have to check. Here, again, your local Small Business Development Center should be able to help. You can also check at your city hall or county offices.

Naming and Licensing Your Business

Your business must have a name. It can be your name or part of your name with or without other elements, or it can be entirely made up, with no reference to your name.

If you have already decided on a business name—your own or an assumed or fictitious name—you need only determine what your legal requirements are (more on this follows) and how you should go about fulfilling them. If you're undecided, a helpful exercise is one writers and editors use when searching for just the right title. They list the possibilities and examine their merits. Let's take a look at how such a list might shape up for someone named Terry Johnson, who's trying to name a home-based craft business. Here are some possible combinations:

1. Terry Johnson
2. Terry Johnson Crafts
3. Terry Johnson, Master Crafter
4. Johnson's Crafts
5. Johnson's Craft Studio
6. Terry Johnson's Craft Shop
7. Terry Johnson's Crafts Unlimited
8. Terry Johnson's Craft Factory
9. Handicrafts by Johnson
10. Johnson's Craft Shop
11. Terry Johnson's Woodcraft [or other craft] Studio
12. Johnson and Company
13. Terry Johnson and Associates
14. Terry Johnson Arts-and-Crafts Enterprises
15. Crafty Creations
16. The Craft Factory
17. The Craft Company
18. The Arts & Crafts Factory

See how it works? By listing all the names that occur to you and switching elements about, within minutes you will have a working list. In an hour you could probably come up with fifty or more names. Just list as many as appeal to you; then begin eliminating those you like least.

Registering Your Business Name

Before picking a name for your business, you'll need to learn about any legal restrictions. Depending on state law or local ordinances, you may or may not have to register your business name; even if you're not required to do so, you may want to. Visit your local Small Business Development Center or chamber of commerce and ask for information about registering a business name.

Where I live, a person who uses what the rule writers call a *real and true name* as a business name need not register the name or pay a filing fee. A real and true name is defined as a person's surname with the given name or initials. My real and true name is Kenn Oberrecht, Kenneth Oberrecht, G. Kenneth Oberrecht, or G. K. Oberrecht.

My state also permits the entrepreneur to add descriptive words to the real and true name without its becoming an assumed business name, which must be registered. If you add certain words that imply additional owners, however—such as *associates, company,* or *sons*—you may have to register it as an assumed name, as is the case in my state.

Let's take another look at the list of possible names for Terry Johnson's business and assume Terry has moved to Coos County, Oregon, and wants to set up a home-based business. Put a check mark by each of the listed names that won't require registration.

Numbers 15 through 18 are obviously assumed names and must be registered. Of the remaining names, numbers 4, 5, 9, 10, 12, and 13 would also require registration.

Even though number 14 would not require registration, it's a terrible business name. It's too long. Shortened to Terry Johnson Enterprises, it would still escape registration requirements but would then be too vague.

Mistakes to Avoid

In naming your business, avoid vogue words, slang, and clichés. Don't be too cute. There's nothing wrong with a good catchy name, but a fine line divides catchy business names from cutesy ones.

Stay away from names that are too obscure or esoteric for the general public or any that are otherwise inappropriate. The Bit & Blade might mean something to you but could be meaningless to most of your potential customers. Aardvark Aarts will probably get you listed first in the Yellow Pages but might also detour prospective customers who haven't the slightest notion of what kind of business you run.

You want your business name to be remembered. It should be easy to say and easy to spell. If you have a name like mine, I strongly recommend paying the filing fee and adopting an assumed business name.

Don't let your business name limit you. Johnson's Clock Shop meets all the essential criteria for a good business name, but what happens when Terry gets interested in marquetry or wants to expand into making toys, jewelry boxes, and wooden bowls? The name becomes obsolete.

Craft is a broad term that might not be quite specific or descriptive enough for some home-based businesses. Slight modification, however, can make it useful and direct. Johnson's Woodcraft tells the potential customer that here's a business that sells products made of wood, which can include anything Terry is interested in creating. Terry can also branch out into other areas of woodworking without fear of making the business name obsolete.

Licenses and Permits

When you visit the Small Business Development Center or local government offices, inquire about any requirements for licenses or permits. You might need some kind of paper issued by the state, county, or city you live in.

In Alaska I had to be licensed by the state. In Oregon there's no such state requirement. I live in a community consisting of the side-by-side cities of Coos Bay and North Bend. In Coos Bay I would have to have a business license; in North Bend I don't.

There's usually a small annual fee associated with business licenses or permits. Failing to be properly licensed, however, could cost you a stiff fine or even put you out of business.

Hiring a Lawyer

These days, lawyers are like ears: Most of us have one on each side. So it would seem that finding a lawyer would be as easy as turning left or right. But, like ears, not all lawyers are good ones.

Do You Need a Lawyer?

The important question is, do you need a lawyer? Let's hope you never will, but the odds are against that likelihood. Americans are the most litigious people in the world. No wonder—we represent only 5 percent of the world's population, but we have 75 percent of the world's lawyers.

Do you need a lawyer? Probably. Do you need one right now? Probably not, but you should keep one handy. That means you must find a lawyer with a good reputation, make an appointment, and discuss your plans. There should be no charge for this initial meeting, and you should feel no obligation toward the lawyer or law firm. If for any reason you're uncomfortable or uneasy with this lawyer, try another. In fact, you might want to meet with several before deciding which one would be ideal as your legal adviser.

Finding the Right Lawyer

The best way to locate prospective lawyers is to ask around. If you know other artisans and entrepreneurs in your community, ask who their lawyers are and if they're satisfied with the service they're getting. You can also check the Yellow Pages of the phone directory under "Attorneys—Referral," or phone your local Small Business Development Center. There's probably a toll-free number available for the state bar association, which may have a referral service.

Many lawyers specialize, so you can narrow your choices by eliminating those prospects who work primarily in areas irrelevant to your needs, such as probate, divorce, juvenile, mortgage, immigration, bankruptcy, or personal-injury law. Look instead for a lawyer with a general practice and experience in contract and business law. The same lawyer will probably be able to handle your personal legal matters as well. Should the need for a specialist arise—say, for someone versed in patent law—your attorney will probably be able to refer you to a competent colleague.

Insuring Your Home-Based Business

An insurance agent should be more than someone who peddles policies and collects commissions, so you will have to shop around for the right agency and the right insurance companies. I use the plural *companies* because you will need several policies and might have to deal with more than one company. Independent agents, however, write policies for various companies, so it's possible to work with one agent for all your insurance needs. In any case, you should review your insurance requirements and policies annually and compare prices.

Will Your Homeowner's Policy Suffice?

Your homeowner's or renter's policy may or may not cover your business. That's the first thing to find out. Even if it does, there may be limits to the coverage on some expensive equipment. For example, some tools and other equipment might be covered, but for only a few hundred dollars. So you will want to list certain items and get additional coverage for them. You may need a rider on your policy to cover your business as well as your home and all its contents.

Vehicle Insurance

There was a time when most of us took out a vehicle policy and stayed with the same company permanently. Policies were nearly identical and rates were similar. Not so now. Rates and coverage can vary considerably from company to company. So look around and remain alert for better deals.

If you have a good driving record and you're tired of paying high premiums to cover the people who don't, do as I did several years ago: Tell your agent you want a better policy with lower premiums. If your agent can't offer you lower rates, find a company or agent who will. Be aware, though, that some of these companies will offer attractive rates to get your business, then after a year or so will start increasing your premiums until you're right back where you started. That's when it's time to go shopping again.

People used to look for a company that offered good coverage on a vehicle policy, would not drop a client merely for having a chargeable accident, and would pay claims promptly and adequately. Now many companies will drop you in a blink, and you can count on claims hassles and a fight for every nickel owed you. So if you're going to get stuck with that kind of service, why not pay the lowest possible rates?

Do You Need Extra Liability Insurance?

Liability insurance is expensive, and that included in your homeowner's or renter's policy might not be adequate for your business. If you plan to sell products from your home and will have customers, clients, or even delivery people coming to your property, you'll probably need extra liability coverage, so discuss that with your agent.

Disability and Health Insurance

If you're young and healthy, you should probably consider disability insurance. The older you get, and the more health problems you have, however, the higher the premiums will be. In fact, they quickly rise to prohibitive levels.

Similarly, the younger and healthier you are, the cheaper your health insurance will be. Regardless of your age or condition, though, as a self-employed person you can count on paying the highest premiums for the poorest coverage. Some professional associations offer group rates for their members, but don't expect any terrific bargains. From the standpoint of health insurance, your best prospect is to be married to a working spouse whose employer offers good family coverage.

Life Insurance

Life insurance is a complicated matter about which few generalizations are possible. You must assess your own situation to determine what kind of coverage, if any, you want or need. If your death and the loss of income from your craft business would create financial hardship for anyone, you probably need some kind of life insurance policy, either term or whole life. Talk to your agent about it.

Finding an Insurance Agent

Find an insurance agent the way you would find an attorney or accountant: Ask others for recommendations. Talk to several agents and pick the one who seems to know the most about the insurance business and can assure you of looking out for your best interests. Keep in mind, though, that every insurance agent is first and foremost a salesperson; your best interests are secondary.

Trademarks, Patents, and Copyrights

Most businesses are made up of physical property and intellectual property. Physical property includes business assets, such as office equipment, furniture, machinery, computer software, and vehicles. Intellectual property consists of company and product names and logos, inventions, and designs, as well as artwork, photographs, audiotapes, videotapes, films, and most written material.

We take many measures to protect our physical property. We see to routine maintenance and repairs. We lock doors and windows and may even install expensive security systems. We also insure our property against fire, theft, and other risks.

None of these precautions, however, adequately protects intellectual property. For that purpose we must use trademarks, patents, and copyrights—three distinctly different proprietary terms that share some characteristics.

Trademarks

A trademark is a name, logo, symbol, word, or graphic representation that a business uses to distinguish its products from those of other businesses. A company's services are similarly protected by a form of trademark known as a *service mark*.

The superscript symbols ™ and SM are used to identify trademarks and service marks that are not federally registered. The symbols serve notice to the public that common law protects whatever bears those symbols. When a business registers a trademark or service mark with the U.S. Patent and Trademark Office (PTO), it should then identify its product or service with the symbol ®, which designates federal registration.

You can register your trademark in your state or any state where you do business. It's a relatively easy and inexpensive process you can do yourself. Start by writing to the state attorney general's office and requesting the proper application form. Registration fees run from about $10 to $100 and probably average about $25. To protect a logo, product name, or service name, make sure you always include the proper trademark or service mark and note the date of its first use, which you will need to furnish when applying for other trademark registration.

If at any time you use or plan to use your trademark or service mark in interstate commerce, experts recommend you then file for registration with the PTO. In addition to the completed application form, you must submit a drawing of your trademark or service mark, three specimens of the mark as it is used in commerce, and the filing fee. A letter or phone call to the PTO will get you the proper forms and a copy of the booklet *Basic Facts about Trademarks*.

There's a good chance that state registration and common-law protection will suffice, in which case you won't have to register your trademark with the federal government. Even if you engage in interstate commerce, you may file for registration on your own, without hiring an attorney. I recommend, however, that you at least discuss the matter with your attorney, who should be able to determine how complex your trademark is and if you will need further legal assistance. Even an attorney who's not a trademark expert can recommend one who is.

Trademarks last from five to ten years, after which they must be renewed to remain registered and protected.

Patents

A patent is an exclusive right a government grants to an inventor, a manufacturer, or an authorized representative to make, use, and sell an invention for a prescribed amount of time. In the United States a patent lasts for fourteen to seventeen years and is not renewable.

Persons engaged in the crafts business needn't be concerned with patents and patent law unless they have invented objects or created designs they think might be patentable. To pass the test of patentability, new inventions and designs must meet certain criteria, among them usefulness and utility. They also must fall into one of five statutory classes: (1) processes, (2) machines, (3) manufactures, (4) compositions of matter, or (5) new uses of any of the above.

Two of the three types of patents available in the United States are of potential interest to inventive artisans: utility patents and design patents. Utility patents, good for seventeen years, apply to new inventions. Design patents, which last for fourteen years, are for unique shapes or designs of existing types of objects.

If you have an invention to patent, you may prepare the application yourself, file it with the PTO, and represent yourself in the patent proceedings. But the process is extremely complex and time consuming. What's more, even if you are granted a patent based on an application process you completed unaided, it might eventually prove to be inadequate protection for your product or design.

My brother Phil is a founding partner in a busy Boise, Idaho, law firm. His practice includes a good bit of trademark work. He has worked to secure trademarks for his clients throughout the United States and in such far-flung places as Singapore and Sydney, Australia. When a client needs patent work done, however, Phil hires a patent attorney in New York.

If you want to patent something, I suggest you follow the good example of Phil and others and hire a patent attorney or patent agent. To practice before the PTO, a patent attorney must also hold a degree in engineering or physical science. A patent agent must have the same technical or scientific expertise and must pass the same examination patent attorneys take. A patent agent is not a lawyer, however, and therefore cannot represent a client in patent litigation.

Your attorney can probably recommend a patent attorney or agent or may elect to work with one in representing you. The PTO also maintains a directory of registered patent attorneys and agents. Check for a copy at your local public or college library.

Even if you plan to hire an attorney, I suggest you read the booklet *General Information concerning Patents,* available from the U.S. Government Printing Office and possibly at a local library. Armed with the information contained in the booklet, you'll be able to ask your attorney intelligent and pertinent questions.

If you insist on trying to secure a patent on your own, then you will want to read *Patent It Yourself,* a hefty but readable book by patent attorney David Pressman.

Copyright

Copyright is a form of protection for original works that authors, poets, playwrights, composers, choreographers, artists, photographers, and other creators enjoy. It is afforded more or less automatically to any work, immediately on its creation in fixed form, and the copyright in the work normally becomes the property of the author or creator. In the United States, as of January 1, 1978, copyright lasts for the life of the artist or creator plus fifty years.

Filling out a form and paying the necessary fee to the U.S. Copyright Office does not copyright a work. Copyright is part and parcel of the creation process. If you create a work in fixed form, it is copyrighted and you own the copyright, unless you were an employee of a company and that company paid you to create the work, or you were not an employee but created the work under the terms of a work-for-hire agreement. Filing the paperwork and paying the fee *registers* the copyright.

There is no requirement to register a copyright, but it's best to do so as a way of claiming your copyright. Registration helps immensely if you ever need to sue someone for copyright infringement.

Copyright is available for unpublished and published works. It protects all unpublished works. It protects virtually all published works created by U.S. citizens and most foreign residents in the United States, as well as citizens of foreign nations that are signatories of one of the various copyright treaties to which the United States is also a party.

Among the various kinds of copyright-protected works, those you are most likely to create, use, or come in contact with in your business are literary works, photographs, graphic works, maps, audiotapes, videotapes, and computer software.

Some material is not eligible for copyright, including ideas, procedures, principles, names, titles, slogans, short phrases, lettering, familiar symbols, and typographic ornamentation. Most government-prepared material is also in the public domain and cannot be copyrighted.

Mere ownership of a work does not grant or imply copyright to the owner. Unless otherwise agreed upon in writing, copyright belongs to the *creator* of the work.

To illustrate, let's say there's a local artist whose work you particularly admire. As part of your business you buy lithographs of the artist's paintings, which you then mount, mat, frame, and sell at regional arts-and-crafts fairs. As the buyer, you legally own the prints. The people who buy the framed prints from you then legally own them. Both you and your customers are bona fide owners of the lithographs and may keep or dispose of them in any way, including selling them for a profit. But neither you nor anyone else may legally *copy* or *reproduce* the prints in any way without the artist's written consent. Regardless of the disposition of the lithographs, the artist retains the copyright.

Before 1978, to be copyrighted, most works had to be published with an acceptable copyright notice. Although virtually all works, published or not, are now protected, publication with the proper copyright notice is still important.

The Copyright Office defines publication as "the distribution of copies . . . of a work to the public by sale or other transfer of ownership, or by rental, lease, or lending." If you produce any kind of work that's eligible for copyright protection, it should bear the proper copyright notice.

As of March 1, 1989, use of the copyright notice became optional; before then it was mandatory. I recommend you follow the practice, however, because it offers certain distinct advantages. A copyright notice shows the year of first publication, which is an important reference. It identifies you as the owner of the copyright, and it serves notice to the public that the work is protected.

Moreover, if the copyright is infringed but the work carried the proper notice, the court will not allow a defendant to claim ignorance. Damages awarded might be as high as $10,000 per infringement, and in some cases could be up to $50,000. You may successfully sue for infringement even if the work did not bear copyright notice, but the claim can be deemed "innocent infringement" and result in greatly reduced damages—perhaps as little as $100.

A proper copyright notice has three important elements: (1) the copyright symbol ©, or the word *Copyright*, or the abbreviation *Copyr.*; (2) the year of first publication; and (3) the copyright owner's name. Example: Copyright 2003 Kenn Oberrecht.

Under the old Copyright Act of 1909, works could be copyrighted for twenty-eight years; then copyright could be renewed for another twenty-eight years, for a total of fifty-six years. For any copyrights in effect on January 1, 1978, the renewal term has been increased to forty-seven years, affording maximum copyright protection of seventy-five years. But such copyrights *must be renewed.*

Once a copyright expires, the work or property is in the public domain and may be freely used by anyone. Prior to January 1, 1978, improper copyright notice or failure to use a copyright notice on first publication often rendered works public domain.

Of the various ways to protect intellectual property, registering a copyright is the easiest. Filing the forms is not a complicated or tremendously costly process, and many of us do so without the assistance of an attorney. If I discovered someone infringing my copyrights, however, my first action would be a phone call to my attorney.

For additional information on copyright, visit your local public library. The Copyright Office will also send you a packet of publications on copyright, as well as the proper forms and instructions for registering copyright. (See the "Source Directory" at the back of this book, under "U.S. Government.")

Contracts

A contract is an enforceable agreement between or among two or more parties, permitting or prohibiting certain actions and activities, with mutual but not always equal benefits accruing to each party. Contracts of some form or another are used in most businesses.

Agent or Representative Agreements

If you plan to work with an agent or representative, you probably will be asked to sign an agreement stipulating that for each sale the agent makes, a share of the selling price (usually 10 or 15 percent) goes to the agent.

Traveling to the various trade shows is expensive, so agents representing artists and artisans often charge a nominal fee for each show. Details should be spelled out in the contract.

Agents also like to include exclusivity clauses in their contracts, which means that you agree to sell your works only through that agent or that you agree to pay the agent's percentage even on works you sell without the agent's help. This is a one-way clause I don't like. My response to such a clause is, "Fine. I'll be happy to agree to the exclusivity clause, provided we amend it to say that you will devote your full-time efforts to selling my work exclusively and will not represent any other artist or artisan as long as you are representing me."

Of course, no agent will agree to such a preposterous clause, but it makes the point and sets a foundation for negotiation. Try to get any such clause deleted, severely restricted, or rewritten in such a way that it poses little or no difficulty for you. You don't want to get tied into a restrictive contract, for as long as a year, with an agent who turns out to be a lazy jerk.

Other Contracts

Some artists and artisans use work orders or job orders to set up contracts with their customers. These are simple forms that you fill in with all the pertinent information and customer's stipulations. They should be imprinted with your conditions and stipulations.

When the customer signs the order and receives a copy of it, you and the customer then have a contract for a specific job.

You can have a local printer print work orders and other contract forms, make your own forms, or order them by mail. NEBS, Inc., has a number of such forms available and will imprint them with your name, address, and phone number. If you don't find one that fits your needs, NEBS will custom-print contract forms for you. (See the "Source Directory" at the back of this book, under "Direct Sales Outlets: Business and Office Equipment and Supplies.")

Get Help

If you aren't accustomed to working with contracts, and you find their language baffling and full of unnecessary obfuscation, note all the confusing and confounding clauses. Then take the contract and your notes to your attorney for a translation. Pay close attention to what your attorney tells you, and soon you will learn to understand contracts without having to pay someone to interpret them for you.

Chapter Six

Writing a Business Plan

Abusiness plan is your blueprint for success. It's not something you devise and abandon once you're in business, but rather a working, changing, growing document and the basis for all your forecasting and goals.

A business plan is a detailed scheme describing how a proposed or existing business conducts its operations. In a home-based craft business, it's a strategy, worked out in advance, designed to define and delineate the ways the owner/manager will finance, operate, and profit from the business.

Your business plan can also be a document to use for attracting financial backing or selling your products and services to potential clients. Moreover, it can help you establish credit and credibility.

I had been operating my business full time for five years when my wife and I decided to build the house we now occupy. My financial planning and forecasting helped me to prepare a convincing document that ultimately led to qualification for a home mortgage with a very attractive interest rate. It enabled me to expand my business from a small office and workshop to a comfortable and spacious work complex of about 1,200 square feet.

Drafting a business plan requires careful thought, effort, and time. Don't try dashing it off over a weekend. Take the task seriously and give it the time it needs.

I must confess that when I started my business, I did not have a written business plan. I had a good idea of what I wanted to do and how I intended to accomplish it. Over the years I had also given a lot of thought to the business. I had studied, spent years in college, and researched the areas my college courses hadn't covered.

I'm not sure a written plan would have made a great difference in the early, part-time years of my business. Nevertheless, I'm convinced that a formal plan would have forced me to consider aspects of the business I had ignored and would have alerted me to potential problems I could have averted.

For most prospective entrepreneurs, the toughest part of writing a business plan is getting started. If you've read the first five chapters of this book and followed the directions there, you have already begun putting your plans and ideas on paper, and you should realize by now that it's not such a difficult process.

Writing a business plan is challenging and sometimes difficult, but it can be an enjoyable and enlightening exercise that hones your problem-solving skills and provides a foundation on which to build your business.

Why You Should Write a Business Plan

Of the various reasons for writing a business plan, not all apply to the home-based artisan. During the early stages of your operation—perhaps for the life of your business—you needn't worry about mergers, acquisitions, attracting highly skilled employees, or setting up strategic alliances with major corporations.

Your reasons for developing a good plan are more fundamental and pragmatic. Your plan should enable you to do the following:

- *Assess the feasibility of the venture.* You will eventually have to convince others that your home-based craft business is or will be a healthy, viable operation. The first person you must convince, though, is yourself. A good business plan is the most persuasive tool at your disposal for that purpose. In the final analysis, you'll be able to determine whether you should start your own business or keep your day job.
- *Evaluate your business resources.* Listing all your physical assets and professional attributes will enable you to determine what your needs are and where your strengths and weaknesses lie. This can serve to reassure you and others and to steer you down the right road.
- *Evaluate your financial resources.* Before going into business, you must know what your financial status is and where you'll acquire needed operating capital. You

should also have resources to fall back on in case of an emergency or in the event of an investment opportunity.

- *Identify potential customers.* You must know who your clients or customers will be to market your services and products to them most effectively. You need to identify your immediate buyers and target your future buyers.

- *Establish a workable timetable.* Once you have determined that your venture is feasible and evaluated your resources and markets, all that's left is to decide when to open your business. Also make some flexible decisions about growth and progress by plugging future plans into your timetable.

- *Set reasonable and competitive fees or prices.* How will you bill your clients or charge your customers? What do other local artists and artisans charge? You'll need to research fee and price structures thoroughly to ascertain what your services and products are worth and include that information in your business plan.

- *Provide a framework for scheduling.* Time study and scheduling are crucial to business success. You must know not only what any given project or product will cost you to produce, but also how much time it will take. Both short-range and long-range scheduling will continue as integral, ongoing processes for the life of your business.

- *Create a basis for forecasting.* Related to the scheduling process is a form of guessing known as forecasting. To forecast business trends, cash flow, and profit margins requires intelligence, experience, a thorough understanding of the competition, a firm grasp of markets, and a top-quality crystal ball. In the absence of the last-mentioned item, a good business plan is a reasonable substitute.

- *Facilitate the setting of realistic goals.* A business without goals is a trip without a destination—a time-consuming, money-wasting, aimless wandering. It's important to set goals from the start, and as you realize them, to set new ones. Your goals shouldn't be too easily attained or impossible to achieve. They must be on the tough side of realistic.

- *Land important and lucrative jobs.* If you have an opportunity to bid on a corporate or government job, the people letting the contract will want to know all about you and your business. You'll look like a bush-league player if you don't have a confidential business plan ready for limited distribution.

- *Secure bank or investor financing.* Although it's best to avoid borrowing money to run your business—especially during the formative years—you could experience a temporary cash-flow interruption or might need to buy some expensive equipment in order to land a job. A business plan can go a long way toward securing needed funds.

Organizing Your Business Plan

I can't offer you any rules or formulas for preparing a business plan. Just as no two businesses are entirely alike, no two plans can be identical. Business plans vary greatly, even within the same industry.

There's no set length or established format for a business plan. It can be as detailed or as abbreviated as you want to make it. Business plans for major companies might run to forty pages or more. I've heard of some reaching a hundred pages. Yours will certainly be shorter—probably somewhere between ten and twenty pages. But don't consider this absolute. Make it whatever length you're comfortable with.

As you begin listing information for your plan, include as many details as you can. Make the rough draft as long as it needs to be without padding. Then work it down to as precise and concise a document as possible.

Remember, a business plan is a working document about your operations; it should change as your business does. Consequently, it is not something that simply amounts to filling in the blanks on a form.

Business-plan forms are indeed available from several sources. You'll find them in books on business and publications from the Small Business Administration, as well as in handouts from your local Small Business Development Center. There are even computer-software programs available. All these sources—including this chapter—are only guidelines, designed to help you write your own business plan.

Every business plan should be neatly typed or printed on good-quality bond paper, with 1-inch margins top, bottom, left, and right. Plans prepared with a computer are best printed with a laser or ink-jet printer.

Your business plan should have a cover page and a table of contents. It's also a good idea to include an executive summary. Other important sections should address such topics as organization, finances, management, and marketing. If you wish to include such ancillary documents as a résumé or brief autobiographical statement, credit references, and letters of recommendation, put them in an appendix at the end of the plan.

The plan should be divided into sections, with each section titled according to contents: Executive Summary, The Organizational Plan, The Financial Plan, and so on. Divide the sections with subheads.

Make sure everything about your business plan is as perfect and readable as you can make it. Misspelled words, misplaced punctuation, shabby sentence and paragraph structure, and errors in grammar and syntax leave a mighty poor impression. The implication is that if your business plan is sloppy, maybe your business practices are too.

If you're among the legions who have trouble handling the mechanics of American English, hire help. Find someone who can read your finished plan, locate the errors, and correct them. You'll need a consultant with above-average skills. Keep in mind, though, that just because someone teaches high-school or college English or works as a writer or an editor doesn't necessarily mean that person is an expert in style, usage, and the mechanics of contemporary American English. In fact, finding such a person may well prove the most difficult part of creating your business plan.

Don't try to impress people with big or fancy words or with how much you happen to know about business or crafts. Avoid jargon, clichés, and buzzwords. Keep the language straightforward, simple, and clear.

Even if you are a skilled writer who doesn't need outside help, have someone read your plan and look for those elusive typographical errors and the little obscurities that make a sentence or paragraph cumbersome or awkward. Your plan should be pleasant and easy to read.

Cover Page

Center the phrase *Confidential Business Plan* at the top and bottom of the cover page, preferably in large boldface type. This is a message to anyone who reads or refers to your plan that the contents are not for general distribution.

About a third of the way down the page, center your business name, street address, P.O. box if you have one, phone number, fax number if you have a dedicated fax line, e-mail address, and Web address if you have a site.

CONFIDENTIAL BUSINESS PLAN

Arts & Crafts Unlimited
1492 Columbus Drive
Moon Valley, IN 54321
Phone: (123) 555–4545
Fax: (123) 555–6767
E-mail: tjohnson@homenet.com
Web: www.artsandcrafts.com

Proprietor: Terry Johnson

Copy Number _____

CONFIDENTIAL BUSINESS PLAN

Then number each copy you distribute, for whatever reason. Keep a log in your business-plan file that lists every person who receives a copy of your plan, the number on that copy, and the date of distribution. This is another important message to anyone in possession of your business plan. It lets people know that you are keeping tight control of this document and implies that the recipient is responsible for safeguarding its contents.

Table of Contents

Provide a table of contents as a convenience to the reader. Simply list the various sections of your plan and their corresponding page numbers.

Executive Summary

Like the table of contents, the executive summary is provided as a convenience to your reader. Your business plan covers all aspects of your business in detail. The executive summary covers the same subjects, but in brief form. Try to distill the essence of your business into one page, with perhaps a paragraph each devoted to the major sections of your business plan.

The executive summary is a courtesy to anyone who will be reading or referring to your business plan for whatever reason. In the minute or so it takes to read this one-page abstract, the reader can determine whether or not to read on or study the plan more closely. That makes it an extremely important part of the business plan.

Like the lead to a magazine article or news story, the executive summary must be as interesting, informative, and relevant as you can make it.

The Organizational Plan

The organizational plan is where you lay out the specifics of your business organization. Start by identifying yourself and your business as a sole proprietorship, partnership, or corporation. Your home-based craft business will doubtless begin as a sole proprietorship, and chances are it will remain in that status.

If you have one or more persons working with or for you, include that information. Note whether these are full-time or part-time, permanent, or temporary employees or associates. Discuss their contributions to the operation of your business. If they're family members, mention that too.

You need to explain why your business exists and how it functions. Discuss its strengths, your business philosophies, and your craft skills. Resist any temptation to get technical.

Provide a clear picture of where you stand as you plan to launch your business and where you *intend* (don't use the word *hope*) to be a year from now, two years from now, and five years down the road. Demonstrate that you have immediate objectives and long-range goals. Write about the scope and direction of your business, and indicate what your scheduled operating hours and days are.

The Financial Plan

The financial plan is the most important part of your business plan. That's why two chapters in this book are devoted to financial planning and management. If you have read Chapters 3 and 4 and prepared the financial documents covered there, you have already done most of the work required for this section of the business plan.

Statement of Financial Condition

Begin the section with a brief narrative statement of your financial situation, followed by a statement of financial condition, also known as a *personal financial statement or statement of net worth.* (See Chapter 3, under "The Personal Financial Statement.")

For the beginning entrepreneur, this is the only part of the financial plan that can be precise. The rest of it is an educated guess at best, but you'll be called on to make such guesses more often than you might think, especially by lending institutions, the Internal Revenue Service, and probably your state revenue agency.

Sources of Funds

The Sources of Funds section is the place to divulge your financial sources.

The adage "It takes money to make money" applies to every business. You can't expect to attract clients or customers if you haven't carefully and wisely invested in assets and made plans to capitalize your business. What's more, investment and capitalization are continuing processes, lasting as long as you remain in business.

The chief function of a business plan is to provide an accurate appraisal of your business's financial health. This information will enable you to secure loans or entice financial backers; it should also make financial management easier for you.

Include a short report in your business plan called "Sources of Funds," which should list your assets, their worth, and their sources, as shown in the accompanying sample.

The Capital Assets Inventory form is handy for compiling the figures you'll need. Use a separate form for each type of property listed: furniture and fixtures, office equipment, shop equipment, studio equipment, and craft equipment. You need not include these forms in your business plan, because you'll summarize their contents under "Sources of Funds."

The completed inventory forms, stored with your insurance policies, are valuable documents should you ever experience a casualty loss, so it's important to update them regularly. If you must list or schedule certain property for insurance purposes or carry all-risk coverage for your equipment, be sure to send a copy of the appropriate form to your insurance agent each time you update it.

Sources of Funds

Assets	Amount/Cost	Sources
Cash	$3,000	Business Savings
Investments	$15,000	Certificates of Deposit
Accounts Receivable	$2,000	Business Sales
Materials and Supplies	$1,500	Currently on Hand
Vehicle	$14,000/$17,500	Installment Purchase
Furniture and Fixtures	$1,300	Currently Owned
Office Equipment	$5,200	Currently Owned
Studio Equipment	$400	Currently Owned
Workshop Equipment	$8,300	Currently Owned

Capital Assets Inventory

Type of Property _____   Date of Inventory _____

Description	Serial Number	Date Acquired	Cost or Value

TOTAL VALUE _____

Capital Assets Inventory

Type of Property Workshop Equipment   Date of Inventory January 31, 2003

Description	Serial Number	Date Acquired	Cost or Value
Black & Decker Power Miter Saw	078539	1984	$ 185.00
Black & Decker Industrial Bench Grinder	001594	1985	125.00
Black & Decker Sander/Grinder	001138	1987	100.00
Elu Router and Router Table	EBD61493	1988	300.00
Toolcraft 4¼" Joiner/Planer	TCX5329	1990	275.00
Craftsman 10" Table Saw	SC88423	1990	400.00
Craftsman Belt and Disk Sander	SC00324	1991	275.00
Craftsman 13" Drill Press	SC01438	1992	225.00
Craftsman 10" Radial-Arm Saw	SC63115	1999	500.00
Assorted Power Tools			2,000.00
Assorted Hand Tools			2,500.00
Blades, Bits, and Accessories			1,500.00
Tool Cabinets			600.00

TOTAL VALUE _____ $8,285.00

Profit-and-Loss Projection

For the purposes of your business plan, prepare a profit-and-loss projection for the upcoming year on a monthly basis, then quarterly for the second year, and annually for the third, fourth, and fifth years. (For details, see Chapter 3.)

If you are starting your business in midyear, project the remaining months of that year on a monthly basis. If you start your business in October, for example, you should project profit and loss on a monthly basis for the first five quarters (or fifteen months), then quarterly and annually as described above.

Remember, a business plan is a living, working, evolving document. It should be a five-year plan that you review and modify as necessary—but at least once a year.

Balance Sheet

People accustomed to working with balance sheets will no doubt want to see one in your business plan. Prepare one according to the directions in Chapter 3.

Cash-Flow Projection

A cash-flow projection will probably prove to be one of your more useful financial documents, so you should include one as part of your business plan. (Consult Chapter 3 for details.) You might also want to discuss how you use profit-and-loss and cash-flow projections to manage the financial aspects of your business.

The Management Plan

In the Management Plan section, you must demonstrate your ability to manage your operation. Various business publications stress the importance of the team concept of management. They insist you list the various members of your management team and devote a half page each to a description of each member's strengths and management experience.

How Many Ponies in Your Show?

If you have other key people in your organization, by all means describe them. In your home-based craft business, however, you probably represent the entire management staff and labor force.

There's nothing wrong with the one-pony show, provided the star attraction isn't just a one-trick pony. So here's where you will need to tell about your show and all the tricks you know. You'll need to discuss your experience and diverse skills. Talk up your abilities and explain how your business will profit from them. I'm not suggesting you embellish the facts, merely that you uncover them and use them to your best advantage.

Discuss Your Skills and Experience

In courses I've taught, I have worked with students who thought they had no valuable experience to build on, nothing worthwhile to offer. A brief one-on-one conference or interview, however, invariably turns up hidden talents and attributes.

To help you prepare a brief narrative statement, refer to your résumé, or make a list of the jobs you've held and duties you were responsible for. Be relevant. Zero in on jobs and duties that demonstrate management skills.

For instance, if, when you were a high-school or college student, the state highway department hired you in the summer to pick up roadside litter, that's not relevant. On the other hand, if you were put in charge of a crew of summer workers picking up litter, that shows you have supervisory experience and indicates that you can handle responsibility.

If you have valuable craft experience, describe that too. Include amateur as well as professional work. Mention any awards, exhibits, or special recognition you've received.

You should even include any relevant volunteer or pro bono work and organizational offices you've held. All of this contributes to your business and personal identity and defines who and what you are.

List Your Business Associates

Even if you are the sole proprietor of a one-person operation, you have or should have professional or business associates you ought to list in your business plan. Provide the name, address, and phone number of your insurance agent, banker, accountant, lawyer, and any suppliers you work with.

Deal Intelligently with Your Weaknesses

Of course, you'll want to elaborate on your strengths as a manager and artisan, but you should also identify your weaknesses and describe the actions you'll take to eliminate them.

For example, if you plan to use a computer in your business and you've had plenty of computer experience, that's a strength worth discussing. If you have had no computer experience, perhaps you plan to take a course or two at a local computer center or community college. Or maybe you plan to learn on your own with books, videocassettes, and tutorial software.

Weaknesses and insufficiencies are nothing to be ashamed of, but if you ignore them or fail to plan for their elimination, they remain an impediment to progress and success. Merely planning sensibly to shore up a weakness can neutralize its effect for the time being. Taking action as planned can turn a weakness into a strength.

The Marketing Plan

The first step in drafting a marketing plan is determining what, exactly, your business will provide its clientele in the way of products or services. You have probably already determined that. If not, you must do so now.

Identify Your Competition

Deciding what your craft business will sell will help establish your niche in the marketplace. Knowing this makes it easy to identify your competition and how you will deal with it.

Identify Your Markets

Developing a sound marketing plan requires market analysis. You need to conduct some methodical but fairly simple research to determine who your potential customers are and how many are out there.

If you intend to sell your products through local and regional galleries and gift shops, you need only determine how many such outlets there are in your area of operation to arrive at a base figure. You might also talk to the gallery and shop owners to get an idea of the number of customers they deal with monthly or annually.

If you intend to sell your craft items at arts-and-crafts fairs and other exhibits, show promoters should have figures available on how many people have attended previous shows and how the exhibitors have fared.

Perhaps you plan to sell your products through established mail-order sources. Any such company that accepts your products can provide figures on catalog distribution and order generation.

If an agent agrees to accept your work and represent you, ask for sales figures. Find out how many shops and galleries you can expect to do business with and how many trade shows the agent will attend. Gather as much pertinent information as possible and extrapolate the data as best you can.

The more numbers you can gather, the easier it will be to identify your potential markets and assess their worth.

Determine Your Market Share

Determining your market share is a bit more difficult, but, because it mainly requires guesswork, your figures can't easily be challenged. Be realistic and conservative in your estimates, and you'll probably outperform your best guess.

You will surely find that you don't have the capacity to take full advantage of your potential market share. For example, if you plan to sell through gift shops, galleries, and other retail stores and consider any such establishment within a day's drive to be in your range of operation, you might well discover 500 or more such outlets in your territory. How many of those do you think you could supply? Half? A fourth? A mere 10 percent would be fifty businesses and probably a more reasonable target. In fact, you may well find that to be more business than you can handle.

How many arts-and-crafts fairs are there annually within your territory? Find out, and while you're at it, determine which are the best. In the beginning you may have to hit them all as part of the learning process and in order to get your name and products known. Eventually, however, you will probably settle on several shows that consistently prove to be your best moneymakers.

Shortly after I moved to Oregon, I met and became friends with a high-school art teacher who moonlighted at regional arts-and-crafts shows. He wanted to quit teaching and devote himself full time to setting up and running a home-based business. When he decided to make the plunge, he continued selling his work mainly at regional shows.

For the first couple of years, he hit about a dozen shows a year, which is an exhausting, nearly impossible pace to maintain, but meanwhile he was able to make a living and build a mailing list of more than 10,000 customers. Ultimately, he settled on the three shows a year where, each autumn, he made about 75 percent of his annual income. He continued to work these shows while nearly doubling his mailing list. Now he's able to devote the first three quarters of the year to creating and developing products, running the lucrative direct-mail side of his business, and preparing for his show season.

His marketing plan was a good one. Not only has it enabled him to establish a smoothly running home-based business where he's his own boss, but in the meantime he has also gotten rich.

Your marketing plan should boil down to a fair assessment of the marketplace, how you will compete, who your potential customers are, what your market share amounts to, and how you will deal with growing demands on your business. After seeing to the necessary research and market analysis, put all this into narrative form and include it in your business plan.

Appendixes

You may or may not wish to include appendixes. If you have sterling credentials, though, you should seriously consider putting them into your business plan.

This is the place to include your résumé, a list of where you have exhibited and sold your works, a list of business and personal references, a list of credit references, and copies of letters of recommendation or commendation. If you have collected more than a few awards for your craftworks, make a list and include it here.

Chapter Seven

Taxes and Record Keeping

These days, it seems tax collectors are coming at us from every direction. Depending on where you live and do business, you may have to pay city, state, and federal income taxes; self-employment tax; personal-property and real-estate taxes; city, borough, county, or state sales taxes; state and federal fuel taxes; room taxes; and an assortment of other taxes disguised as user fees, license fees, application fees, registration fees, permit fees, and filing fees.

You will need to determine the kinds of taxes you must pay in your city, county, and state. If you don't already know, check with your local Small Business Development Center, chamber of commerce, or the local office of your state revenue department.

All of us must pay federal taxes, which we'll discuss momentarily. Because circumstances vary, even among people who are in the same business, and because tax codes and their numerous supporting documents exist in a constant state of change, it's impossible to provide specific advice. Furthermore, in the space of a chapter, I can provide only an introduction to taxes and taxation. I'll try to pass on some helpful tips and give you a good enough grounding in the concepts so that you will be able to continue on your own.

In dealing with your taxes and essential record keeping, you can be involved at any level you wish, ranging from doing it all yourself to hiring others to do most of it for you. In any case, you need to understand what your responsibilities are. Even if you decide to turn everything over to someone else, you will still have to see to some tax chores.

Your options are several. You can do your own bookkeeping or hire a bookkeeper. You can prepare your own tax returns and associated forms and schedules, or you can have a professional tax preparer, accountant, certified public accountant, or attorney do it for you. The choices are yours, but I am going to make some recommendations.

First, keeping books is relatively easy, so I suggest you do it yourself, especially the first year or so you're in business. This will not only help you contain start-up costs, but it will also introduce you to the fundamentals of record keeping.

I continue to do my own bookkeeping after all these years because it helps me stay in touch with the financial aspects of my business and lets me know how I'm doing from month to month. What's more, a bookkeeper would be one more person I'd have to deal with in my busy life, and I'd rather not just now. Besides, by the time I've collected and sorted all my receipts, bills, canceled checks, and such, all that remains is entering the information on ledger pages and running the numbers through my calculator. With the right software you can even do it all by computer. It's no big deal.

I'm not about to tell you that doing your own taxes is easy. Far from it. It's a tedious, often confusing, sometimes infuriating task that just seems to get a little worse every year. Nevertheless, I recommend you try your hand at it as a way of learning about taxation and how it affects your business. I won't carry this recommendation too far, however. Once you've had the experience, decide for yourself whether to continue on your own or hire help. Learning how to keep books and prepare your tax returns will enable you to provide better, more complete information when you decide to turn it all over to someone else.

The tendency of most Americans is to put off tax chores as long as possible. Don't join the herd, especially if you decide to try preparing your own returns. You probably won't have all the documents you need until the end of January, so spend that month gathering all your essential forms, schedules, publications, and antacid tablets. Plan to work on your returns in February. That way, if you find you need help or discover that you don't have all the necessary documents, you'll have time and won't need to panic, or worse, pay a penalty for filing late.

Using Your Home as a Business

As a home-based crafts professional, you should be able to take a tax deduction for any rooms you use *exclusively* and *regularly* for conducting your business. These can include an office, a studio, a workshop, a storage room, a gallery, or combinations thereof. A studio, for example, need not be used exclusively as a studio but must be used exclusively as part of your business. My studio is a multipurpose room that houses my studio equipment, but it also has a desk and worktable where I do sorting and filing and see to much of my mounting, matting, and framing. Most of my reference books are on the bookshelves that line two walls of my studio. Along another wall are filing cabinets. So this room functions as a studio, library, and storage area, while serving other business purposes as well.

If you're planning to use only a portion of the space in a garage, basement, attic, or other large open area for business purposes, you might consider partitioning it to take advantage of allowable tax deductions. For example, you could partition off a room to use exclusively as an office or office-studio combination, thereby enabling you to take a business deduction for the square footage of that room, even though the remaining area may be used for personal or household purposes.

Another possibility would be to convert a spare room into a home office and partition off one corner of a basement or garage to set up a workshop. You could then take a deduction for the square footage of your office and workshop.

Similarly, you can take a deduction for a room you use for storage. You cannot simply put up shelves or cabinets for business storage in a room you use for other personal or household purposes, then take a deduction for that space. You can, however, partition off that space to create a separate room, thus making that square footage eligible for the deduction.

Use Test

You may be entitled to limited deductions for the business use of your home, but such use must meet certain criteria.

Exclusive Use

That portion of your home used for business must be used exclusively for such purposes in order to qualify for a tax deduction. You can't use a room as a studio, sewing room, and guest quarters, then claim a business deduction for it or any portion of it.

Regular Use

To meet the regular-use criterion, you must regularly use a specific part of your home for business, but "regular use" has more to do with continuity than frequency. For example, you might set up a well-sealed, dust-free, and adequately ventilated room as your paint room. Although you may work in your shop or studio every day, you might have products ready for painting only once a week or once a month. Provided that you use the paint room for no other nonbusiness purposes, it should be as eligible for a deduction as the shop or studio you use every day.

Principal Place of Business

Determining your principal place of business is a potential source of confusion. If you are a full-time home-based crafts professional, your home should qualify as your principal place of business, and the space you have set up for doing business should be eligible for a limited deduction. If you have a shop, studio, or gallery downtown, however, and decide to set up an office at home for seeing to various business tasks, your home office probably would not be eligible under the current regulations, because it is not your principal place of business.

Interestingly, though, the IRS recognizes the fact that you can have more than one principal place of business, provided that you're engaged in more than one business. For instance, if you teach carpentry full time at a local community college and work weekends out of your home as a wood-carver, you could have two principal places of business: the college, where you are in the full-time teaching business; and your home, where you are in the part-time craft business. So you should be able to take the home-office deduction, so long as you meet the other criteria. Or you could be a lab technician, motorcycle mechanic, chef, plumber, cop, or computer programmer five days a week and run a part-time craft business from your home and still qualify for the deduction.

Separate Structures

The IRS also allows deductions for separate freestanding structures, such as a detached garage, barn, studio, shop, or storage building, provided that it's used exclusively and regularly for business. If you have any such structures on your property, they might suit your purposes. Keep in mind, too, that as your business matures, it might outgrow its space. Separate structures could prove the ideal solution to that problem.

Trade or Business Use

According to the IRS, "You must use your home in connection with a trade or business to take a deduction for its business use." Your home-based craft business should easily meet this criterion.

Calculating Your Business Percentage

The allowable deduction for operating a business from your home is based on the percentage of total home space your business occupies. It's a simple matter of arithmetic:

1. Determine the square footage of your entire home.
2. Determine the square footage of your business space.
3. Divide the square footage of your business space by the total square footage of your home; the result is your business percentage.

Example: Let's assume you live in a two-bedroom apartment of 750 square feet and convert a 10-by-15-foot bedroom into a home office and studio. Multiply the room dimensions to arrive at the square footage (10 feet x 15 feet = 150 square feet). Now divide the square footage of the converted bedroom by the total square footage (150 divided by 750 = .20). Your allowable deduction is 20 percent. If you live in a house of 3,000 square feet and use 1,000 square feet for business, your allowable deduction is 33.33 percent. You see how it works.

The IRS allows you to use any reasonable method to determine your business percentage. The one I've described is the most accurate and is certainly easy enough.

What You Can Deduct

Expenses associated solely with your living quarters and other areas of your property that have nothing to do with your business are *unrelated expenses* and as such are not deductible. These include repair and maintenance of living quarters and most appliances, landscaping expenses, lawn care, and such.

If you need to repair or replace a dishwasher or range, no portion of the associated costs is deductible. On the other hand, some seemingly unrelated expenses might be deductible. For example, if the furnace that heats your entire home breaks down, part of the repair or replacement bill should be deductible, according to your business-deduction percentage.

Costs associated solely with the benefit of your business are known as *direct expenses* and are fully deductible. If you put new carpeting in your office, paint your studio, or hang a new light fixture in any part of your work area, you may deduct the expense.

Most of the costs of running and maintaining your entire home are partly deductible as *indirect expenses.* They include mortgage interest, real-estate taxes, utilities, trash-collection fees, some telephone charges, insurance premiums, and the cost of installing and maintaining security systems.

Casualty losses, depending on their effects, can be unrelated, direct, or indirect expenses and are accordingly deductible or not. A grease fire that damages only your kitchen is a casualty loss but is unrelated to your business and is not an allowable business deduction. If a storm blows the windows out of your office, the casualty loss is directly related to your business and is fully deductible, less any insurance compensation. If a tornado delivers your roof to an adjacent county, the loss affects both your business and living quarters and is treated as an indirect expense, less any insurance or other reimbursement.

If you're a renter who meets all the criteria for the business use of your home, the business percentage of your rent is deductible. If you're a homeowner, however, no portion of your principal payments on your mortgage is deductible, but you should be able to recover these business costs over several years by taking an annual deduction for depreciation of the building and any permanent improvements to it.

Limitations and Reporting Requirements

Your allowable deduction, including depreciation, for the business use of your home is limited. In the simplest terms, deductions for the business use of your home are not allowed to exceed your net income. If they do, all or part of the deductions might be disallowed for that year, but those disallowed expenses may be carried over to a later year.

Form 8829, Expenses for Business Use of Your Home, is where you report all this information and where you will determine whether or not your expenses for any given year are deductible that year.

Using a Vehicle in Your Business

It's hard to imagine running any home-based business without using a vehicle. Depending on the nature of your work, you may need to drive only occasionally, or you could be on the road every day. You can buy a vehicle to use exclusively for business purposes, or you might enlist the family flivver for both business and personal use.

The IRS uses the term *car* to mean any passenger vehicle that does not exceed 6,000 pounds gross vehicle weight. That includes the kinds of vehicles most of us use for transportation: automobiles, vans, minivans, pickup trucks, and sport-utility vehicles.

Near Home and Away

Depending on the kind of craftwork you do and where you sell it, you might travel only locally or cover some distance to see to your business needs. Your business-home area includes the metropolitan, suburban, or rural area where you do business during the course of a normal workday. If you travel to and from a business location within the same day, that's considered local use of your vehicle, and costs associated with such use are deductible as *vehicle* expenses.

If business takes you away from home overnight or for a longer period, you must consider your vehicle expenses to be part of your *travel* expenses, which are recorded and handled separately and reported in a different section of Schedule C, Profit or Loss from Business.

According to the IRS, expenses for the local business use of your vehicle are deductible "if the expenses are ordinary and necessary. An ordinary expense is one that is common and accepted in your field of trade, business, or profession. A necessary expense is one that is helpful and appropriate for your business. An expense does not have to be indispensable to be considered necessary."

Vehicle Use Test and Expense Records

If you use a family vehicle for both business and personal purposes, business mileage must amount to more than 50 percent of the total mileage to qualify for the highest depreciation deductions. So you must keep good mileage records. How else could you know that of the 18,500 miles you drove last year, 12,580 were for business, allowing you to deduct 68 percent of your vehicle-operating costs?

You should keep a mileage log, but it needn't be anything elaborate. Note the date and odometer mileage when you place a vehicle in service. Also record the odometer reading on January 1 each year. Then for each trip, write down the date, destination or purpose, starting odometer mileage, ending mileage, and total mileage.

Your log can be a notebook or a ruled pad on a clipboard that you keep in your vehicle. You can also make your mileage log part of your business planner and calendar, either with loose-leaf pages or printed pages designed for such purposes. Printed vehicle logs are also available at office-supply outlets.

You may elect either to take a standard deduction for each business mile you drive or to deduct actual vehicle expenses and depreciation. In the latter case, you should also keep receipts, work orders, canceled checks, and any other documents that substantiate your claims for expense deductions. You're not required to keep a separate diary or journal of vehicle expenses, but you may do so if you prefer that to recording expenses in a general expense ledger. In either case, you need not duplicate any information already contained on your receipts and other documents.

Mileage vs. Expenses

Whether to take the standard mileage deduction or deduct actual operating expenses is up to you. If your vehicle is inexpensive to operate, you might be smart to take the mileage deduction. You'll probably be better off deducting operating expenses and depreciation, however, if you drive an expensive gas hog.

In addition to keeping a mileage log, I recommend you record all your operating costs as well for the first year. At tax-filing time, do all the necessary calculations for both methods and pick the one that will give you the greater deduction.

Once you have determined the total miles and business miles driven for the year, divide the business miles by the total miles to arrive at your business percentage. For example, if you drove 10,935 business miles and 3,645 personal miles, total mileage for the year was 14,580. If you divide 10,935 by 14,580, you'll find that your business miles constituted 75 percent of the total. That means you can deduct 75 percent of your operating expenses and depreciation, or multiply the standard per-mile deduction by 10,935 and deduct that amount.

Leasing a Vehicle

Another option is to lease a vehicle instead of buying one. With a leased vehicle, you are normally allowed to deduct maintenance and repair bills, operating expenses, and lease payments. You may not use the standard mileage deduction, nor may you deduct for depreciation. You also need to log business and personal mileage.

Depending on the kind of lease agreement you sign, the IRS might require you to treat the leased vehicle as you would a purchased vehicle. If your lease contains an option-to-buy clause, the IRS may consider this a purchase agreement. So be careful with any lease and its wording. You may wish to seek assistance from the IRS or your attorney before signing a vehicle lease.

If the vehicle you lease has what the IRS considers an "excess fair-market value," you will also have to report an "inclusion amount" when you file your tax return. For information about all this, see IRS Publication 463, *Travel, Entertainment, Gift, and Car Expenses*, or one of the commercially available tax guides published each year.

Mileage Log

Date	Destination/ Purpose	Starting Mileage	Ending Mileage	Total Miles

Total Miles This Page _____

Renting a Vehicle

Should your business require you to travel away from your business-home area by public conveyance, such as by plane or train, you might need to rent a vehicle once you reach your business destination. Your rental payments and operating costs are deductible as travel expenses, as are your plane or train tickets.

Other Deductible Expenses

Unless you take the standard mileage deduction, most expenses you incur while operating your vehicle for business purposes are deductible. In addition to fuel, repairs, and maintenance, they include but are not limited to bridge and highway tolls, ferry fees, parking fees, parking-valet gratuities, and towing charges, should your vehicle become disabled.

Fines for moving and parking violations are not deductible, nor are towing charges that stem from illegal parking.

Using a Computer in Your Business

If you buy a computer that you and other family members use for personal reasons, schoolwork, computer games, and other nonbusiness purposes and you also plan to use it for business, the IRS considers this *listed property*, and you will need to keep track of and distinguish between personal and business use. If your business use is less than 50 percent of the total use, your deductions will be limited.

Logging computer use is more difficult than logging vehicle use, especially if several people use the computer. For that reason and others, I recommend you purchase a computer, put it in your office or studio, and use it exclusively for business. In this case, it is not considered listed property, and you may treat it as any other depreciable business property.

All peripheral computer equipment and hardware and most software are also depreciable property. Blank diskettes (floppy disks) and compact discs (CDs), computer paper, printer ribbons or cartridges, labels, and other essential computer materials are deductible as office supplies. (For more information on computers, see Chapter 8.)

Business Expenses

Most of the costs of running your business are fully deductible in a straightforward way. As the sole proprietor of a home-based business, you will have to sort out the various deductions and report them on their respective forms: some on Form 8829, Expenses for Business Use of Your Home; some on Schedule C, Profit or Loss from Business; and some on Form 4562, Depreciation and Amortization.

We've already discussed deductions for the business use of your home and will more fully discuss depreciation later. For now, let's take a closer look at the kinds of expenses you will report on Schedule C. They include expenses incurred for advertising, business operation of a vehicle, interest paid, legal and professional services, materials and supplies, rent, leases, repairs and maintenance, taxes, licenses, permits, travel, some meals and entertainment, dues to professional associations, some publications, printing and photocopying, postal costs, freight, express and parcel services, trash collection, and others you'll no doubt discover.

Keeping Receipts

Keeping receipts is not the odious chore so many people think it is. It's mainly a matter of developing the habit of collecting receipts for all your business purchases.

For most of your expenses, receipts are automatic by-products of your various transactions. Your telephone, utilities, and other monthly bills are receipts you'll need to keep. When you gas up your vehicle, keep the credit-card receipt; if you pay cash, ask for a cash receipt. When you're on the road, get receipts for all your food, lodging, and other expenses.

If you buy office and craft supplies in quantity, you'll keep the number of receipts to a minimum. Set up accounts with vendors and you'll also save time and trouble by paying and filing monthly statements.

Even when you get all this under control, you will still occasionally need to buy some supplies at supermarkets, drugstores, and discount outlets. Just make sure you get a cash-register receipt. Many register receipts itemize purchases, and all provide dates and amounts. When you get a register receipt that doesn't display all the essential information, fill it in yourself, immediately.

I make a habit of marking receipts as I get them and noting any important information. I use a red pen to circle the date and amount paid. If the receipt isn't itemized, I write down what it was for: hardware, varnish, glue, paper clips, lunch, and so on. This helps me zero in on the information I need when I do my bookkeeping.

When I pay my stacks of monthly bills, I note the date and circle the amount paid, but I don't bother writing the check number on the bill, because that will be in my check register if I need it. While I'm at it, I put a red *X* in the check register at each check I write that goes to pay for an expense for which I don't have an adequate receipt. The canceled check is then my receipt.

No matter how careful you are, you will sometimes forget to ask for a receipt, or you might lose one. In that case, make your own receipt at once, noting all the pertinent information. This should be acceptable to the IRS. What's important is that you write the receipt while everything is fresh in your mind, not at the end of the month when you do your bookkeeping.

Depreciation of Business Property

The purchase of certain equipment, tools, furnishings, and other property you use in your business is considered a capital expenditure, not normally eligible for deduction as an expense for a given tax year. Rather, it must be treated as depreciable property, with the cost deducted gradually over a number of years. Normally, this includes any property that has a useful life of more than one year.

In addition to vehicles and computers, already discussed, other depreciable property you will probably use in your home-based craft business includes the following:

- *Furniture and fixtures* for your office, studio, and workroom.
- *Office equipment,* such as a calculator, copier, fax machine, or telephone.
- *Craft equipment,* including power tools, sewing machines, kilns, and such.
- *Buildings* not used for residential purposes, including the business portion of your home.

Property Classes and Recovery Periods

Depreciable property is classified according to the number of years you must normally take to depreciate it or write it off. Because of the conventions you're required to use in calculating depreciation, recovery periods run a year longer than their respective classifications. For example, so-called five-year property will remain on your books for six years, seven-year property for eight.

Any machinery you use—including office and workshop equipment, computer equipment, and vehicles—is five-year property. Desks, chairs, filing cabinets, bookcases, tables, and other furniture and fixtures you use in your business are seven-year property.

Congress keeps extending the recovery period for nonresidential real property. In 1993 it was increased from 31.5 years to 39 years. By the time you read this, it could be even longer. The annual deductible rate for 39-year real property is 2.5641 percent, except for prorated first and last years.

Section 179 Deductions

Section 179 deductions are an exception to what we've been discussing. Certain tangible personal property used in business is eligible to be treated as an expense and may be fully or partly deductible for the tax year. You may deduct up to $24,000 of the cost of such property as office equipment, craft equipment and machinery, computers, and computer peripherals.

Your business vehicle is eligible, provided it was not previously used as a personal vehicle and then converted to business use. The Section 179 deduction for qualifying vehicles is also limited.

Buildings are not eligible for Section 179 deductions.

You can use this information to your advantage by paying close attention to your earnings and expenses. If you have a better year than you anticipated, you might need all the immediate deductions you can legally take to reduce your taxable income. This is a good time to look for possible 179 deductions. If your income turns out to be lower than you expect and you have plenty of deductions, you probably won't want to take the Section 179 deductions, even if you have purchased eligible property. Normal depreciation procedures will extend your deductions into future years, when, presumably, your income will be higher.

Reporting Depreciation

Enter all pertinent depreciation information on Form 4562, Depreciation and Amortization. Once you have calculated your allowable depreciation, enter the total on Schedule C.

Surmounting all the obstacles and wading through the mire of instructions for figuring depreciation can make for a difficult trip. This single aspect of taxation may be troublesome enough to make you seek the services of a tax professional.

If you want to try it on your own, you should consult IRS Publication 334, *Tax Guide for Small Business*. Some of the commercially available guides, such as *J. K. Lasser's Your Income Tax* and *H & R Block Income Tax Guide,* are much more readable and relatively free of bureaucratic gobbledygook.

Estimating Your Taxes

Uncle Sam does not like to have money owed to him at the end of the year, so we're required to keep our taxes paid up. Under a simpler, saner system, it would be easy to do the bookkeeping at the end of the month, deduct a reasonable percentage from profits, and mail the old guy a check. But Uncle also dislikes simple and sane systems. So we have yet another form to fill out and file quarterly and another exercise in exasperation.

If you're working part time at this business and full time elsewhere, you can increase the amount your employer withholds from your paycheck to keep from owing taxes at year-end. You could have a working spouse do the same, if you file jointly. Otherwise, you will have to estimate your income and taxes, file Form 1040-ES, and pay your estimated taxes quarterly.

Filing the forms is the easy part; figuring out what to put on the forms is the hard part. When you first encounter this obstacle, you'll ask the same question the rest of us did: How can I possibly know what I'm going to earn in the future? Then you'll do what the rest of us did: Guess.

If you've worked at your business part time, you can use your records to extrapolate income and expenses and at least come up with a figure.

Safe Harbor

IRS regulations provide what is known as a "safe harbor" for estimating taxes and avoiding penalties. As of 1994 self-employed individuals with prior-year adjusted gross incomes of $150,000 or less are permitted to base their estimated-tax payments on 100 percent of their prior-year tax liability. Those with adjusted gross incomes exceeding $150,000 may base their estimations and payments on 110 percent of their prior-year tax liability.

You are not required to use the safe harbor, but if you elect not to, your estimated-tax payments for the current year will have to equal at least 90 percent of your prior-year tax liability. Otherwise, you could be charged a penalty.

Record Keeping

As a self-employed taxpayer, you may use either the accrual or the cash accounting basis. With the accrual basis, you report income as it is earned, not as it's received. You also report expenses on the dates you incur them, not necessarily on the day you pay them. With the cash basis, you report income when you are paid and costs as you pay them.

Advantages of Cash Basis

Cash accounting is definitely the simpler method. It also offers certain advantages that can save you tax dollars. For example, at the end of a high-income year, you may elect to delay your billing until late December or early January in order to defer payment of money owed you into the coming tax year, thus reducing your taxable income for the current year.

No Set Rules for Records

You must keep accurate records of all your income and all your expenditures. There are no set IRS requirements, however, for how you set up your books, as long as you maintain written records or computer records you can print out.

You can turn over your record-keeping chores to a professional or do them yourself. You might want to visit an office-supply outlet to examine available commercial accounting and record-keeping systems, or you could devise something yourself. If you own a computer, you may wish to review some of the many software programs available for business and personal financial management and record keeping.

A Simpler Bookkeeping System

I use a simple manual bookkeeping system I devised when I first went into business part time. It has served me well for years, keeps me informed, and is housed in a single three-ring loose-leaf binder, which is organized with index-tab pages. The ledger pages are created from my handy-dandy four-column pads.

To keep track of income, I label the top of a page *Income,* followed by the year. The narrow left column is labeled *Date,* the wide column *Source,* and the four accounting columns, respectively, *Amount, Month, Total for Month,* and *Cumulative Total.*

As checks arrive I enter the date, source, and amount. At month's end I write the month in the second column, income for the month in the third column, and a running cumulative total in the fourth column. I record all reimbursed expenses the same way on a page that's identical except for the title.

For recording most of my expenses, my ledger has index tabs and pages labeled *Vehicle, Office, Repairs & Maintenance, Dues & Publications, Photo Supplies, Shop Supplies, Printing & Photocopying, Postal, Freight & Shipping,* and *Miscellaneous.* For each of these categories, I prepare the page with *Date* in the far left column and *Item* in the wide column. I then label the four accounting columns *Cost, Month, Total for Month,* and *Cumulative Total.*

Several categories call for special handling. For example, my *Travel & Entertainment* pages reflect certain IRS requirements as well as my own need to see how I spend my money. I label the four accounting columns *Meals & Entertainment, Transportation, Lodging,* and *Miscellaneous.* After each trip I subtotal each column. The IRS allows a deduction for only a percentage of meals and entertainment, which the ledger page keeps separate.

On another page titled *Utilities, Phone, & Trash,* I label the wide column *Month,* under which I list the twelve months. The four columns are for *Electric, Water, Phone,* and *Trash.* Totals for electric, water, and trash get adjusted by my business percentage. I adjust my phone charges as I review my monthly bills.

If you have only one phone line coming into your home, the IRS does not allow a deduction for that line but does allow the deduction of long-distance business calls. If you put a second phone line or a dedicated fax line into your office, you may deduct charges for that.

I have four insurance policies that are directly or indirectly related to my business. The insurance page in my ledger has columns for *Vehicle, Boat, Homeowner,* and *Mortgage.* I report costs for my vehicle and boat insurance on Schedule C, adjusted homeowner's and mortgage insurance on Form 8829.

For depreciation, I make ledger pages for various kinds of property. Although I could keep all five-year property together and all seven-year property together, I prefer to categorize further. For example, I have pages labeled *Books & Software (5-Year Property), Machinery & Equipment (5-Year Property),* and *Furniture & Fixtures (7-Year Property).* I also keep the records for my business vehicle on a separate page, labeled *Vehicle (5-Year Property).*

The far left column of each depreciation page is labeled *Date,* the wide column *Item,* and the first accounting column *Cost.* I leave the other columns untitled until year-end. If I elect to expense any of these items as a Section 179 deduction, I so note it on the page for future reference. If I depreciate property, I then use the other columns, showing the current year and percentage allowed at the head of column two. The following year I enter the year and percentage at the head of column three, and the year after I use column four. Sometimes there's sufficient room to continue adding the out-years at the bottom of the same page. When there's not, I just add another page.

I try to keep up with all this by doing my bookkeeping monthly, but sometimes I'm too busy and must put off the job for a month or so. At the end of the year, I run my column totals and do all the necessary calculating to make my books ready for filling out my tax forms.

Capitalizing Start-up Costs

To qualify for a deduction of the preliminary costs of starting a business, the IRS requires those costs to be capitalized over time. Some of these costs might not be deductible until the business terminates. All of this can lead to some complicated and time-consuming record keeping.

For big companies making major investments in equipment and materials, the record keeping and procedures are necessary for taking the concomitantly large deductions. For the home-based entrepreneur, however, the puny deductions are hardly worth the hassles.

Income/Expenses

Date	Source	Amount or Cost	Month	Total for Month	Cumulative Total

You can simply elect not to take any deductions for start-up costs. You won't have to do all that bookkeeping, and you won't run afoul of IRS regulations. Just make sure you keep your start-up costs low. Anything you buy before you're in business is the kind of expenditure that would have to be capitalized to be eligible for deduction. Once you've made a sale, however, you are officially in business and may then begin deducting expenses in the same tax year they occur.

Of course, you will want to use tools and materials you already have on hand; you just can't take deductions for them if you want to avoid the capitalization hassles.

My recommendation is to keep your start-up costs minimal and make a sale as soon as possible. Don't buy new office furniture and equipment or lay in large quantities of materials and supplies before you've sold anything. Operate on a shoestring until you make a sale; then begin purchasing the necessities for your business, keeping all the receipts and maintaining careful records of all expenditures.

Sales Tax

Depending on the nature of your business and your state's requirements, you may have to apply for a license to collect sales tax on the items you sell.

If your state has a sales tax, you could be required to collect taxes on items you sell directly to customers at arts-and-crafts shows, craft fairs, and similar events. On the other hand, you probably won't have to collect taxes on items you sell through shops, galleries, stores, or any other retail outlets where the proprietors of those businesses collect taxes from their customers. Similarly, you should be exempt from paying sales taxes on raw materials and finished products that you purchase for resale. The idea here is to prevent what would amount to multiple taxation on the product as it progresses through the stages of manufacture.

You'll need to determine your state's requirements, so check with your local chamber of commerce or Small Business Development Center. You can also get information from your state's revenue department.

Useful Publications from the IRS

Number	Title
17	Your Federal Income Tax
334	Tax Guide for Small Businesses
463	Travel, Entertainment, Gift, and Car Expenses
505	Tax Withholding and Estimated Tax
521	Moving Expenses
523	Selling Your Home
525	Taxable and Nontaxable Income
526	Charitable Contributions
533	Self-Employment Tax
535	Business Expenses
536	Net Operating Losses
538	Accounting Periods and Methods
541	Partnerships
542	Tax Information on Corporations
544	Sales and Other Dispositions of Assets
550	Investment Income and Expenses
551	Basis of Assets
553	Highlights of (the Year's) Tax Changes
560	Retirement Plans for Small Business
561	Determining the Value of Donated Property
583	Starting a Business and Keeping Records
587	Business Use of Your Home
590	Individual Retirement Arrangements (IRAs)
946	How to Depreciate Property

IRS Forms You'll Probably Need

Form	Title
Form 1040	U.S. Individual Income Tax Return
Form 1040-ES	Estimated Tax for Individuals
Form 4562	Depreciation and Amortization
Form 8829	Expenses for Business Use of Your Home
Schedule A	Itemized Deductions
Schedule B	Interest and Dividend Income
Schedule C	Profit or Loss from Business
Schedule D	Capital Gains and Losses
Schedule SE	Self-Employment Tax

Chapter Eight

Using a Computer in Your Business

If you're an intermediate to advanced computer user, you can probably skip this chapter, because you already know more about computers than I do. I'm no computer expert and wouldn't dare pretend to be one. I'm merely a home-based business owner and manager who relies on a computer for an ever-increasing number of business tasks.

If you've had only minimal experience with personal computers or none at all, perhaps I can be of some service. I've learned a thing or two over the years, often the hard way, that may assist you in determining your computer needs.

Like many other busy entrepreneurs, I reluctantly came to the computer world after much deliberation and the discovery of two important reasons for computerizing my business. First, it made good business sense. Second, I was about to be left in the dust by a growing number of computerized colleagues and competitors.

Have I had any regrets about my decision? Only one: that I didn't have the good sense and foresight to make the move years earlier. So learn from my big mistake, allay any fears you may have, and climb aboard—you'll probably enjoy the electronic ride more than you think.

Getting Started with a Computer

The first notion you must dispel is that you need to be a mathematical genius, an electronics whiz, or a nine-year-old child to grasp the intricacies of computer operation. The second notion to put to rest is that a computer is a magic machine that will solve all your business problems.

If you possess enough manual dexterity to operate an electronic calculator or electric typewriter, you can learn your way around a computer's keyboard. If you can read and comprehend at a seventh-grade level, you'll have little trouble learning and understanding the commands essential to the operation of a computer and the functions of hardware and software.

I didn't say you're going to understand, much less enjoy, all the documentation that comes with computer hardware and software. Some of it is written by computer eggheads whose native tongue is jargon and who venture into short phrases of plain English only by accident. You've met them before. They wrote the instructions on how to program your VCR and the manual on how to operate your new auto-everything camera.

The good news is that there are some computer experts who speak and write English and have the ability to translate all that computerese into readable and informative books and magazine articles. Without their help, my own computer would be functioning as little more than an expensive electric typewriter.

A computer won't do much to organize a disorganized business or person. But if your business is already organized and functioning smoothly, a computer can help you keep it that way and save you time in the process.

A computer won't improve your craft skills or make you a better bookkeeper or business communicator. But it can reduce the time it takes to perform tasks associated with your craft and business, thereby freeing you to increase your production or learn more about your craft and business.

While increased productivity is probably the most important benefit you'll gain from computerizing your business, it won't be immediate. In fact, you'll probably lose a few days to setting up your system and learning how to use it. You'll have to spend more time yet mastering the basics and learning what you need to know about various computer applications. You will soon reach a point, however, when you are comfortable with the hardware and software and will begin saving time on various tasks.

What a Computer Can Do for Your Business

In considering the computerization of your home-based business, think of the computer as your assistant manager. You can delegate many tasks to this able helpmate, such as the management of correspondence, accounts, billing, inventory, files, data, money, and time.

You can even assign your assistant all the phone chores, from dialing up customers to answering the phone and routing incoming calls to their proper destinations. It can send and receive faxes and even take messages in your absence. You say you have to leave the office for a while, but you're expecting some important calls? If you own the right software, just leave the number where you can be reached, and your computer will forward your calls. Your computer can communicate with other computers the world over.

You can hook up by modem to on-line services and networks. You can engage in discussions with your colleagues, get answers to your questions, download information, conduct research, buy equipment, and order supplies on-line.

Master the Jargon

When you're trying to learn anything about anything, from aeroballistics to zymology, the first order of business is to master the terminology of the discipline. If you don't know what all the terms, abbreviations, and acronyms mean, you can't expect to learn from what you read and hear.

The computer world is full of jargon, which can be terribly frustrating to anyone trying to learn about computers on an elementary level. I suggest that before you try to read a magazine article or a book about computers, you invest in a good computer-terminology dictionary, such as the *Dictionary of Computer and Internet Terms,* Seventh Edition, by Michael A. Covington et al., (Barron's, 2000) or *Webster's New World Dictionary of Computer Terms,* Ninth Edition, by Bryan Pfaffenberg (Macmillan, 2001).

When you encounter a term you don't understand, look it up. You'll soon be breezing through computer articles and books with no trouble.

Learn by Reading

Armed with your handy-dandy dictionary, you should be ready to learn by reading computer books and magazines. Visit local libraries, bookstores, and magazine stands to see what's available and what might be most appealing and valuable to you and your business. If you have access to an on-line computer, be sure to browse the virtual shelves at amazon. com and barnesandnoble.com.

Well-written books provide an excellent way to learn about computers and software and serve afterward as valuable reference volumes, but you will also need to read computer magazines to keep up with the rapidly changing technology. You'll find a bewildering variety of computer magazines available, but you can narrow the selection by eliminating all the specialized periodicals that deal with hardware and software you don't own, then by examining others to find those you like most.

I recently stopped by a local magazine stand and counted more than three dozen computer and Internet magazines on sale. Of all those, I regularly read fewer than a half-dozen. I like to consult *Computer Shopper* and *Computer Buyer's Guide and Handbook* for advice on buying computer hardware and software. In my attempt, albeit futile, to keep up with technology that advances at warp speed, I haphazardly alternate between *PC Magazine* and *PC World.* One magazine I have come to favor for its clean, uncluttered layout, easygoing style, and fairly jargon-free language is *Smart Computing,* which carries the tag line "In Plain English."

It's probably a good idea to subscribe to a computer magazine, especially if you end up buying several issues a year at ridiculous newsstand prices. The monthly *PC World* and biweekly *PC Magazine* sport cover prices of $6.99 and $5.99, respectively. Pick up a copy of each, hand the clerk a twenty-dollar bill, and you'll get back a mere six bucks and change after sales tax. A year's subscription (twelve issues) to *PC World* costs $19.97, or $1.66 a copy. Subscribing to *PC Magazine* for a year will bring you twenty-two issues for $39.97, or about $1.82 a copy.

What I find particularly valuable in *PC Magazine* and *PC World* are their exhaustive tests of hardware and classes of hardware. The editors of both magazines regularly run tests on desktop computers, notebooks, printers, and other hardware. I bought my first computer system based largely on the testing and evaluation of more than forty similar systems by *PC Magazine.* Keep watch for these issues. You'll learn a lot from them.

Take Computer Courses

One of the best ways to learn about computers is to enroll in basic computer courses. If you don't have the time to spend an entire semester in a course, the intensive one-day or weekend workshops should be more to your liking.

You'll find computer courses offered at local universities and colleges, community colleges, trade schools, computer schools, and some computer stores. Phone or write for university and college catalogs and any literature the trade and computer schools offer. Visit local computer stores to see what they have available and ask to be put on their mailing lists for courses and workshops.

Some computer and software companies also conduct seminars and workshops that can be helpful. Many of these are traveling programs, offered at major population centers in all regions of the United States. Watch for local advertisements and announcements, or phone the companies to inquire about their instructional programs.

Micron Electronics, one of the leading computer companies, has introduced Micron University: hundreds of on-line classes, seminars, and self-paced courses on computer and business topics, available free to Micron owners. I don't see how other major computer manufactures can avoid following Micron's example. More and better-skilled computer users in the marketplace can only lead to greater sales of computers, peripherals, and software.

Befriend a Nerd

Ask my kid brother what he does for a living and he will unabashedly tell you that he's a computer nerd. Actually, he's a musician with his own band and a degree in journalism. He's also a qualified diesel- and small-engine mechanic and a pretty fair carpenter, but his field of expertise is computer and sound-system consulting.

Inasmuch as he resides in Anchorage and I live half a continent farther south, I can pick his brains only by long distance. Luckily, though, there seems to be no shortage of hackers to go around. One friend of mine is an electrical engineer who taught himself to be a computer expert. Another friend is a retired Air Force computer programmer who teaches computer courses and specializes in operating systems, WordPerfect, and navigating the

Internet. He and I live in different cities, but we're able to communicate quickly and easily by e-mail, which also puts me in touch with many other experts.

Chances are you already have at least one friend who knows a lot about computers and software, and you'll surely get to know others who will gladly offer advice. What you learn from these folks can prove invaluable.

You'll also want to find out about computer experts in your vicinity who work as consultants on an hourly basis. Sometimes an hour's worth of a consultant's time can save you untold hours of grief.

Hardware Overview

The basic computer system for a home-based business consists of a keyboard, printer, monitor, and mouse, attached by cables to a case that houses the brains of the whole outfit: the microprocessor, which is an integrated circuit that contains the central processing unit (CPU) on a single chip. The CPU controls the computer and is where instructions are executed and various operations carried out. Also inside the case are the computer's memory and input-output devices.

Microprocessors

The first popular microprocessor was Intel's 8088, which was introduced in 1973. Since then, Intel has introduced succeeding generations of microprocessors that have bested their predecessors in phenomenal leaps, measured in terms of power and speed, or in the amount of data they can process and the speed with which they move it. Other Intel microprocessor designations have been the 80286, 80386, 80486, Pentium, Pentium II, Pentium III, and Pentium 4. The earlier generations are commonly referred to by their abbreviated designations: 286, 386, and 486.

The speed of a microprocessor is measured in megahertz (MHz) or gigahertz (GHz). One MHz is a million cycles per second; one GHz is 1,000 MHz, or a billion cycles, per second. Every instruction takes several cycles. This speed is referred to as *clock speed*. Generally, when measured in terms of identical machine instructions, higher clock speeds result in greater computation speeds. But differences can exist between two microprocessors of the same family, performing the same computations, simply because one computer might be set up differently from the other. In other words, two Pentium III processors operating at 900 MHz might carry out the same instructions at different speeds. Also, succeeding generations perform faster.

As I write this, current-configuration computers sold by the various computer companies are based mainly on the Intel Pentium 4 and the more budget-minded Intel Celeron microprocessors. Although you'll no doubt find plenty of Pentium and Pentium II computers for sale as used equipment, many of these are equipped with hard drives that are too small by today's standards and have insufficient memory (RAM) to adequately handle our many RAM-hungry programs. They may also contain outdated CD-ROM drives, modems, and other hardware. What's more, prices for high-end, if not top-of-the-line, systems are at all-time lows, making the purchase of a new system a better bargain in the long run than the acquisition of even a fairly late model used system.

Memory

Random-access memory (RAM) is among the most important considerations in the purchase of any computer. This is the computer's main working memory and a major determinant of a computer's capacity for accessing program instructions and data. Generally, the more RAM a computer has, the faster and more efficiently it will operate, especially with all the bloated, overfeatured programs we're forced to live with these days.

Modern, graphics-intensive applications gobble up RAM in big chunks. Only a few years ago, computer manufacturers furnished their systems with 8 to 16 megabytes (MB) of RAM as standard equipment, while experts told us we needed at least 32 MB and said that 64 MB was even better for running most Windows-based programs. These days, with the proliferation of memory-hungry programs, most manufacturers offer systems with 128 to 256 MB of RAM as standard fare, with room to expand.

Hard Drives

Just as minimal requirements for power and speed keep increasing, so too does the need for hard-drive capacity. The hard drive is where you will store your applications. If your drive is big enough, you might want to store data there as well.

There was a time when 80 MB seemed a phenomenal capacity for a hard drive, and most of us figured we could get by for years with something so huge. Nowadays a single program can take up 100 MB or more of hard-drive space. We no longer measure hard-drive capacity by the megabyte but by the gigabyte (GB), which is 1,000 megabytes. It's now possible to equip a computer system with an 80 GB hard drive, offering 1,000 times the capacity of that old 80 MB drive.

The experts always tell us to buy a system with as big a hard drive as we can afford. Most desktop systems sold now include big hard drives ranging from 20 to 40 GB. Many computer companies offer upgrades at the time of purchase at attractive prices. Dell, for example, will upgrade a standard 20 GB drive to 40 GB for a mere $20. Upgrades from 40 to 80 GB and from 80 to 120 GB are $70 and $190, respectively.

Diskette (Floppy) Drives

Most computers come with one 3½-inch floppy-disk or diskette drive. A 3½-inch diskette can store up to 1.44 MB, or the textual equivalent of two books the size of this one with room to spare.

Floppy disks or diskettes are fine for saving, backing up, and transferring most unadorned text files and have been used for years for such purposes. For graphics files, digital-imaging applications, and special typographical treatments, as in desktop-publishing applications, larger storage media are essential. Of the various drives and media designed for high-capacity storage—such as the Imation SuperDisk drive, with disks storing up to 120 MB, and the Iomega Zip drive, capable of holding either 100 MB or 250 MB of data, depending on the size of the Zip disk—the medium that has become the most popular and is by far the most economical is the compact disc (CD), with a storage capacity of 650 MB.

CD-ROMs, CD-Rs, and CD-RWs

CD-ROM, which stands for *Compact Disc—Read-Only Memory*, has become so popular and essential that CD-ROM drives, once optional equipment, are now standard on most new computer systems. Compact discs have tremendous capacity: about 650 MB, or more than 450 times that of a 3½-inch diskette. For that reason, all software now comes on CDs instead of diskettes. For the same reason, CDs are a popular medium for storage and transport of digitized images, multimedia presentations, and other bulky files.

With its large capacity and small size, the compact disc offers users one of the best ways to store information in a small space. Recordable CDs, called CD-Rs, sell for as little as 39 cents apiece, and the rewritable CD-RWs sell for under a dollar each, making compact discs the cheapest medium for data storage. Although any ordinary CD-ROM drive can read CDs, CD-Rs, and CD-RWs, you'll need a CD-RW drive (also known as a CD burner) to copy, write, and rewrite compact discs. Such drives are currently standard equipment on many new desktop computer systems and are available as upgrades or optional equipment on others. These upgrades or options are often available for well under $100.

DVD-ROM

DVD-ROM (*Digital Video Disc—Read-Only Memory*) drives are offered as standard equipment on many systems and are available as upgrades or options on others for as little as $50. The DVD was designed to hold an entire digitized, feature-length film on a single disc and has a capacity of 4.7 GB, and larger capacities and applications are promised.

DVD-ROM drives will also read compact discs, although most are not as fast at that task as the highest-speed CD-ROM drives. Combination CD-RW/DVD-ROM drives, two drives in one, are available and enable users to read, write, and rewrite compact discs and read digital video discs. These are standard on some high-end systems and are available as upgrades on others for about $150.

Monitors

Monitor performance is variable among the available models. Video-adapter cards, which are plug-in circuit boards that enable computers to display information on monitors, also affect picture quality. What you need in a monitor-and-video package depends largely on what you want your system to do.

For years the typical desktop computer system came with a monitor that used a cathode ray tube (CRT) to create images on the screen, much like the technology used in television sets. Portable computers, also known as laptops or notebooks, as well as other battery-operated electronic devices, typically use low-power technology called liquid crystal display (LCD) to create screen images. Improvements in LCD technology have led to the development of flat-panel LCD desktop monitors that are much thinner than CRT monitors and take up considerably less space. Flat-panel monitors are standard with some top-of-the-line desktop systems and are available as relatively expensive upgrades or options with other systems. The chief advantage of any flat-panel desktop monitor is that it may fit in tight quarters where the bulkier CRT won't.

Printers

Inkjet and laser printers are the most popular types today, and many makes and models fit the needs and budgets of home-based businesses. Their printing quality is far superior to the older dot-matrix printers. They also run faster and are far quieter. In general, laser printers are more expensive than inkjet printers, but many of the midrange machines are comparably priced. Choosing the right type of printer for your business depends mainly on your needs and expectations.

If you need color capability, you will probably want to invest in the best inkjet printer you can afford, because color laser printers, with prices around $2,000, are out of reach and unnecessary for many of us. If you need to produce large quantities of computer-generated digital images of the highest possible resolution, however, you'll no doubt want to look into the high-end laser printers with color capabilities.

Inkjet printers print by shooting ink onto paper through a matrix of tiny nozzles, with color resolution commonly ranging from 300 to 600 dots per inch (dpi), depending on the machine. With special plastic-coated paper, some inkjet printers are capable of producing images of nearly photographic quality. Printing in black, some inkjet printers approach but don't quite reach laser quality.

Laser printers use electrostatic toner to fuse text and graphic images to paper with tack-sharp resolution of 600 to 1,200 dpi. If you have no need for color and want the best quality text and monochrome graphics, a laser is probably the printer for you.

Whatever type fits your needs, you should be able to find a high-quality, full-featured printer for less than $500. Indeed, some inkjet printers are now priced below $100 and can certainly suffice for the person who has minimal printing needs.

Multifunctional Peripherals

A multifunctional peripheral (MFP) is a machine that performs a variety of tasks. Typical MFPs, available from several manufacturers, operate as printers, scanners, copiers, and fax machines. Although some MFPs cost $1,000 or more, many are priced at half that, or about as much as you might expect to pay for a printer alone. They're also about the size of the average printer. The home-based business manager looking to save money and conserve office space would do well to look into these versatile machines.

The chief criticism leveled at MFPs is that while one unit does the job of four office machines, if it breaks down and must be sent out for repair, the office is left without printing, scanning, copying, and faxing capabilities. Breakdowns are rare, however, and potential downtime only a minor consideration.

A multifunctional peripheral can be a great choice for the start-up home-based business. Even if you don't yet own a computer and don't plan to buy a system right away, an MFP might be your best choice as a stand-alone plain-paper fax/copier. When you get around to buying a computer system, you'll already have a machine to do your scanning and printing.

As with any other equipment, you need to find out what's available, examine the various makes and models for features and functions, and shop around for the best price. (See the "Source Directory" at the back of this book for information on companies that manufacture multifunction peripherals and direct-sales outlets that specialize in computer products.)

Software Overview

Software is what makes a computer work. Without software a computer is useless, incapable of functioning. Software can be divided into three primary categories: systems, applications, and utilities.

Your computer will come with operating-system software, usually the latest version of Windows, already installed. This is the software that controls the computer, manages memory, formats diskettes, and enables the user to create, copy, move, and erase files, as well as run applications software.

Applications software sets up your system to do specific jobs, such as word processing, spreadsheets, accounting, desktop publishing, computer-assisted design, drawing, painting, and digital imaging. With the right applications software, your computer can print all kinds of graphics and forms, see to billing chores, track inventory, address envelopes and labels, create calendars and to-do lists, remind you about meetings and appointments, and help with bookkeeping, taxes, and check writing. Software can teach your system to do calligraphy, sign your name, and even prepare correspondence and other documents in your own digitized handwriting.

Before deciding on any computer system, you must determine the kinds of applications software you want to run; then customize your system around the requirements of the software. Your computer will probably come with some software, and by shopping around you might find package deals with software bundles that include some of the name-brand software you want.

Major software manufacturers, such as Microsoft and Corel, offer their top software titles grouped in "suites" that sell for not much more than any single program in the suite used to cost. With Microsoft Office, for example, you get that company's top-flight applications, including Word (word processing), Excel (spreadsheets), Access (database), Outlook (e-mail, scheduling, and task management), and Publisher (desktop and Web-site publishing). Corel's WordPerfect Office offers the same versatility along with what some of us consider the best word-processing program available.

Regardless of what your individual business and craft needs are, certain categories of applications software are essential to most, if not all, businesses. At the top of the list is word processing. Spreadsheets and heavy-duty accounting programs are essential elements in the corporate world but are often too much for the home-based business, where simpler financial programs are usually better and easier to use. Other programs can help you manage your time and put it to better use.

Utility programs help you maintain and improve the efficiency of your computer and protect it from dangers and nuisances. Common utilities include data-compression, disk-defragmenting, antivirus, and uninstall programs. Many computers come with some utilities already onboard. Some Internet service providers also offer their clients highly efficient utilities that scan for viruses and filter aggravating spam (junk e-mail).

Craft Software

Specialized craft software is a little tougher to locate than the more widely used applications. Nevertheless, with a little digging you should be able to find programs that will make at least some aspects of your craft go a little easier and faster.

Many of the graphics and fonts programs, as well as the so-called draw-and-paint programs, can help create essential graphics for pattern, template, and stencil work. Inexpensive programs exist for needlecraft and craft-related projects. To learn what's available in your craft area(s), read the related specialty magazines and ask your colleagues.

Buying a Computer System

For most of us, houses and vehicles represent our largest purchases. Computers occupy a spot on the list well below boats, motorcycles, lawn tractors, and any number of other expensive items used for work or fun. If we were to evaluate such purchases in terms of complexity, confusion, and frustration instead of cost, however, computers would certainly rank in the top three. For many of us, they would shake out as number one.

Regardless of where you buy a computer system—from a direct-sales (mail/phone/online order) company or local store—you will need to study and evaluate your many options. Even after you've done all your homework and think you know what you need and want, you'll probably experience more than a little difficulty in dealing with all the configurations, combinations, and permutations the various companies offer.

In the search for my second desktop system some years ago, my reading, research, and phone calls eventually narrowed the field to three of the top-rated computer companies. Trying to make intelligent decisions in the face of dozens of configuration options was exasperating. Juggling all the figures and features became remarkably easier, though, when I designed a simple form for comparing the various makes and models.

To use my Computer Systems Comparison, make a copy of the form and fill in your minimum system requirements in the left column. Then make enough copies for all the system configurations you're researching.

On the blank line at the top of the form, write in the brand name and configuration of the system under consideration. Show the configured system's price at the bottom of the

Computer Systems Comparison

_____

	Minimum Requirement	Configured System	Upgrades and Options
Processor			
RAM			
Cache			
Hard Drive			
CD-ROM			
CD-RW			
DVD-ROM			
Monitor			
Modem			
Graphics			
Sound			
Speakers			
Case			
Warranty			
Operating System			
Software			
Extras			
Extras			
Extras			

Configured System $ _____   Shipping $ _____

Upgrades & Options $ _____   Other Costs $ _____

Installation $ _____   Total for System $ _____

Computer Systems Comparison

Dell Dimension 8200

	Minimum Requirement	Configured System	Upgrades and Options
Processor	1.6 GHz Pentium 4	1.8 GHz Pentium 4	
RAM	128 MB SDRAM	256 MB RDRAM	
Cache			
Hard Drive	20 GB	40 GB	
CD-ROM	48X Max.	48X Max.	
CD-RW	16x/10x/24x	16x/10x/40x	
DVD-ROM			
Monitor	15"	17"	
Modem	56 KB	56 KB	
Graphics	16 MB ATI Rage	64 MB GeForce 2	
Sound		Integrated Audio	Turtle Beach: $60
Speakers	Surround/Subwoofer	HK395 & Subwoofer	
Case	Mini Tower	Mini Tower	
Warranty	1-Year on-site	1-Year on-site	
Operating System	Windows XP	Windows XP	
Software	Office Suite		MS Office XP: $150
Extras			
Extras			
Extras			

Configured System	$ 1,399	Shipping	$ 95
Upgrades & Options	$ 210	Other Costs	$
Installation	$	Total for System	$ 1,704

form. In the center column fill in the system's standard hardware, software, peripherals, and features. In the right column list any upgrades and options of interest and their cost. Then it's a simple matter of running the figures, adding shipping and other costs, and arriving at a total system price.

You'll be amazed at how this simple form helps you sort out the profusion of confusion that accompanies the purchase of a new computer system.

Computer and Software Sources

After spending a little time with computer magazines, contact the manufacturers of those computers that seem best suited to your needs. If you have access to an on-line computer, visit the companies' Web sites to review product lines and specifications. Otherwise, phone the companies on their toll-free lines to request literature on their products.

Sources for everything mentioned in this chapter appear at the end of this book in the "Source Directory." Browse through the directory, visit the Web sites, and phone, write, or e-mail for catalogs.

Working the World Wide Web

When the first edition of this book appeared in 1994, the World Wide Web (WWW) was in its infancy. Now it touches our lives in innumerable ways—daily for many of us. For instance, we can read newspapers and magazines on the Web, uncover facts and statistics, get answers to all sorts of questions, find current weather and travel information, research any kind of product or service, download articles and reports on almost any topic imaginable, browse through home pages, and buy or sell practically anything. Nowadays most major companies, national associations, and government agencies, as well as many individuals and small businesses, have their own Web sites.

The World Wide Web is a vast global network of computer sites that publish and disseminate easily accessible information by way of the Internet. Anyone with a computer, modem, and Web browser can access these sites and communicate with them by using what's known as Hypertext Transfer Protocol (HTTP). Reaching any Web site requires no more than pointing a Web browser at it by keying in the appropriate Web address—such as www.craft.com—and tapping the Enter key. Then it's a simple matter of clicking your way through the various pages on that site to find whatever you're seeking. Many Web sites also have valuable links to other related sites.

Web Browsers

Web browsers are programs that run on any on-line computer and come in two types: text-only and graphical. Graphical browsers allow users to view graphics, layouts, and typographical treatments, and so are preferable to text-only browsers. Most new computer systems come with bundled software that includes a graphical Web browser, usually Microsoft Internet Explorer or Netscape Navigator.

You can use your on-line computer and Web browser to access any Web site for which you have an address, such as those cited in the "Source Directory" at the back of this book, in various other printed and electronic directories, in television commericals, and in advertisements in periodical publications. A good site for any craftworker to access and bookmark for future visits is the World of Crafts (www.crafts.com).

Search Engines

In the absence of specific Web-site addresses, you can work the Web and search elsewhere on the Internet by using any of the powerful search engines available to you at no cost. Search engines are programs designed to locate information in databases. Those on the Internet contain mainly World Wide Web information, but some also provide access to other file archives.

Using any of the search engines is a simple and straightforward process, usually amounting to no more than typing in one or two keywords on any topic, then clicking on a Search, Find, or Go button. For example, you might conduct a search on *craft supplies*. The search engine will then look for all documents containing the word *craft* or *supplies*, but will give the highest priority to those that contain both words in their titles, summaries, or texts. There are other ways to conduct searches and specify the results, and most search engines provide Help buttons to coach you through the process. (See the accompanying checklist: 101 Craft Search Topics.)

When you log on to the Internet and launch your Web browser, what first appears on your screen is known as the start page. This is essentially the browser publisher's home page or that of your Internet service provider (ISP), which provides immediate access to one or more search engines. With Microsoft Internet Explorer, for example, msn.com is the default search engine, but Alta Vista, Google, Lycos, and others are only a click or two away. Accessing other search engines requires no more than pointing the Web browser at the appropriate site. (See the accompanying list: A Baker's Dozen Search Engines.)

A Baker's Dozen Search Engines

No search engine is all things to all users. Although a good bit of information overlap exists among them, the various programs often provide different or additional material. Some require distinct search criteria or methods, either readily apparent on the home page or covered under help topics.

While a single search using one search engine may provide all the data you need, sometimes multiple searches are necessary. For example, an initial search that turns up nothing doesn't necessarily mean that relevant information is unavailable on the Internet. Conducting other searches using different search engines often uncovers valuable sources.

After working with several search engines, you will no doubt settle on a favorite that you will use for most of your work. Others will prove especially valuable for specific kinds of searches. For instance, your Web browser's default search engine may give you adequate results and prove to be your fastest route to information. Or you could decide that Google or Lycos serves you better and should be your first choice in any search. If you have specific questions and you wish to phrase them that way, then Ask Jeeves is a good choice.

Most Web browsers also allow users to bookmark favorite Web sites for easy future access, eliminating the need to type the site's address every time. For example, in Microsoft Internet Explorer, once the user has accessed any Web site, bookmarking it requires no more than clicking on "Favorites," then clicking on "Add to Favorites." To reach the site any time after that, click on "Favorites," then on the site designation.

Following are addresses for thirteen of my favorite search engines. Try them out, play around with them, and decide for yourself which are the best for your purposes. To access them, simply point your Web browser at them by keying in their Web site addresses. Then bookmark any or all you may wish to use regularly in the future.

AltaVista www.altavista.com	**Google** www.google.com	**Starting Page** www.startingpage.com
Ask Jeeves www.askjeeves.com	**HotBot** www.hotbot.com	**WebCrawler** www.webcrawler.com
Bigfoot www.bigfoot.com	**Lycos** www.lycos.com	**Yahoo!** www.yahoo.com
excite www.excite.com	**Microsoft Network** www.msn.com	
Go.com www.go.com	**Search IQ** www.searchiq.com	

The Wonder of the Web

The World Wide Web is a powerful and perhaps indispensable research, education, communication, and marketing tool for any twenty-first century home-based craft business. At the very least, it's the best place to get instant answers to questions, find the latest information about craft equipment and materials, and see what other successful craft businesses are producing.

In 1984, according to the U.S. Census Bureau, 8.2 percent of American households had one or more computers. By 2000 that number had soared to 51 percent (54 million households), of which about 80 percent (44 million households) had Internet access. Considering the phenomenal growth of the Web and the number of people with Internet access, the information superhighway could be one of the best research and marketing venues for the home-based craft business.

101 Craft Search Topics

Think of any topic related to crafts, and chances are you'll find an abundance of information about it on the Internet. You need only use one or more of the many various search engines at your disposal and the right search criteria to locate what you need or think you need and probably more than you ever imagined you needed. If the topic has been published or discussed on-line or is available on any accessible database, your computer can lead you to it.

Searches are easy, consisting of no more than accessing a search engine, entering a keyword or phrase, and waiting for your screen to fill with titles and summaries of what exists on the Internet. Some searches require no more than a single keyword, such as *woodworking*, which will provide hundreds, if not thousands, of responses, ranging from manufacturers' home pages, tool and material specifications, product reports, and magazine articles, to bulletin boards, newsgroups, and links to related sites. Other search engines require an extra word or two to make them more specific and confine responses to those that are most pertinent.

Following is a checklist of 101 craft topics or search criteria. Mark those that interest you, add anything else you can think of or for which you need information, and spend some time on a virtual cruise down the information superhighway. You can also refine some of the searches by adding a word or two to what's listed. For example, instead of searching on *candle making* or *wood burning*, you could try *candle making supplies* or *wood burning tools*. Just use your imagination and have fun.

101 Craft Search Topics

- ☐ Adhesives
- ☐ Airbrushing
- ☐ American Indian Crafts
- ☐ Appliqués
- ☐ Artificial Flowers
- ☐ Art Supplies
- ☐ Basketry
- ☐ Batik
- ☐ Bead Crafts
- ☐ Calligraphy
- ☐ Candle Making
- ☐ Caning
- ☐ Cements
- ☐ Ceramics
- ☐ Clock Making
- ☐ Cloisonné
- ☐ Country Crafts
- ☐ Craft Supplies
- ☐ Crochet
- ☐ Cross-Stitch
- ☐ Decorative Crafts
- ☐ Decoupage
- ☐ Decoy Making
- ☐ Doll Clothes
- ☐ Dollhouses
- ☐ Doll Making
- ☐ Dried Flowers
- ☐ Dyeing
- ☐ Embroidery
- ☐ Engraving
- ☐ Etching
- ☐ Fabric Arts
- ☐ Fabric Crafts
- ☐ Fabric Decorating

- ☐ Fabrics
- ☐ Feathers
- ☐ Fiber Arts
- ☐ Finishes
- ☐ Flower Drying
- ☐ Folk Arts
- ☐ Frontier Crafts
- ☐ Furniture Making
- ☐ Glass Crafts
- ☐ Glues
- ☐ Graphics Supplies
- ☐ Jewelry Making
- ☐ Knife Making
- ☐ Knitting
- ☐ Knotting
- ☐ Lapidary
- ☐ Leaded Glass
- ☐ Leather Crafts
- ☐ Lettering
- ☐ Macramé
- ☐ Magnets
- ☐ Marquetry
- ☐ Metal Crafts
- ☐ Metalworking
- ☐ Miniature Making
- ☐ Model Making
- ☐ Mold Crafts
- ☐ Nature Crafts
- ☐ Needlecraft
- ☐ Needlepoint
- ☐ Painting
- ☐ Paper Crafts
- ☐ Paper Making
- ☐ Patterns

- ☐ Photography
- ☐ Picture Framing
- ☐ Pinecones
- ☐ Plaques
- ☐ Plastics
- ☐ Polymer Clay
- ☐ Potpourri Supplies
- ☐ Pottery
- ☐ Quilting
- ☐ Rubber Stamping
- ☐ Rug Making
- ☐ Sandblasting
- ☐ Seashells
- ☐ Seat Weaving
- ☐ Sewing
- ☐ Shrink-Wrapping
- ☐ Sign Making
- ☐ Silk-Screening
- ☐ Spinning
- ☐ Stained Glass
- ☐ Stamp Making
- ☐ Stencils
- ☐ Tackle Making
- ☐ Textile Crafts
- ☐ Tole Painting
- ☐ Toy Making
- ☐ Upholstery
- ☐ Weaving
- ☐ Wire Crafting
- ☐ Wood Burning
- ☐ Wood Carving
- ☐ Woodworking
- ☐ Yarns

Chapter Nine

Managing Your Craft Business

R eading and studying are excellent ways to learn about business management, but you can't learn everything you need to know about managing from books, or even from a four-year college program in business administration. You must also learn from experience, which is another reason for starting your home-based craft business on a part-time basis. Moreover, you should possess certain attributes that are even more important than education and experience.

You can manage a business without formal schooling in business management. You can manage a business without prior management experience. You cannot expect to succeed, however, without common sense and the capacity to think and reason. An indecisive person who has trouble solving problems should forget about starting a home-based business.

Setting Goals

We're often told, sometimes preached at, that as business managers we must set short-term and long-term goals. Well, of course we must. Common sense tells us that no one could expect to run a successful operation without knowing what to do tomorrow, or next week, or three months from now. Continued success depends on knowing what to do next year and the year after. That, simply, is what goal setting is all about. Chances are, you're already involved in the process in a big way. If you're planning to set up your own craft business, you have set a major goal. If you're working on a business plan, you're engaged in both short-term and long-term goal setting.

Setting goals is a fairly simple procedure, not unlike taking an automobile trip. First, determine your destination. Second, pick the best route. Third, pay attention to your progress along the way. Fourth, keep glancing in your rearview mirror so that you'll know what's coming up behind you. Fifth, watch out for the other guy. Sixth, try to stay ahead of schedule without getting in trouble.

Some people recommend setting goals that are easy to accomplish, but I think this is a mistake, especially for the home-based entrepreneur. You should set goals that make you hustle and keep you from succumbing to all the temptations and distractions around the house. In short, set reasonable goals—difficult to reach, but not unattainable.

Job Planning, Forecasting, and Scheduling

In Chapter 4 you learned that the operation of your business, in large part, amounts to the management of money and time. If you properly manage money and time, your business will probably succeed. But that's like saying, if you master the tools and techniques of your craft, you'll probably be a successful artisan. The job isn't quite so simple as it may seem, yet it needn't be the cumbersome exercise many people make of it.

Managing Time

Time management is a matter of knowing everything you have to do and how much time you have to accomplish it, then assigning priorities to most tasks and creating a schedule that allows you to get everything done. Everything. You can't get by with managing only your business time; you must manage all your time to make room for the many jobs, chores, and attendant details in your busy life.

Making Lists

If you're not a list maker, become one. To a greater extent than you might realize, running a business mainly amounts to creating, organizing, and using lists.

1. Every
2. good
3. manager

4. I've
5. known
6. was
7. a
8. list
9. maker
10. .

When making any long-range list of projects and chores, don't dawdle over details. Just empty your mind on paper, minus the minutiae. Assign priorities and see to scheduling later. Begin with the wide-angle view and gradually focus on the close-up details.

Scheduling Work

In my business, I schedule work annually, quarterly, monthly, weekly, and daily. During the last quarter of the year, I usually begin working in my spare time, at a comfortable pace, preparing a schedule for the coming year. As December bears down on me, I pick up the pace so that I can finish the annual schedule before Christmas. Between Christmas and New Year's, I create my first-quarter and January schedules.

I routinely do my quarterly scheduling at the end of December, March, June, and September and monthly scheduling on the last day or two of the preceding month. My workweek runs Monday through Sunday, so I see to weekly scheduling on Sunday evenings. I take care of daily scheduling every evening. That way, I've already planned my workday by the time I get up in the morning.

I lay out my annual schedule by listing, broadly and generally, everything I intend to accomplish during the coming year. This schedule takes the form of several lists in which I group like items: Business Chores, Business Maintenance, Business Correspondence, Capital Investment, and Shopping (craft and office materials and supplies). I also account for demands on my personal time by making similar lists: Personal Chores, House Maintenance, Major Projects, Personal Correspondence, Major Purchases, and Shopping.

Not all aspects of my business end up on lists. Many I just note on my calendar so that I can keep track and take action as necessary. Some are so obvious by now that I don't bother listing them or noting them anywhere. For example, I no longer need to remind myself that my big insurance bills come due in June and December or that the Sheriff of Nottingham will tie his noble steed to my hitching post in November when he comes collecting m' lord's property taxes, or that April 15 is a day that will forever live in infamy in the minds of all Americans. These things I know.

Setting Priorities

My quarterly lists grow out of my annual list, the monthly schedules out of the quarterly ones, and so on. My annual schedule is broad and general, and I assign no priorities to the items on it, other than flagging certain jobs I want to get done in a particular quarter or month. Even my quarterly schedules are fairly free of priority assignments.

My monthly schedule usually contains (1) all the chores, jobs, and projects that *must* be done that month; (2) some that I want to finish that month, if possible; and (3) a few that I'll get to if time permits, but it's no big deal if I don't. Although I don't actually number the items on my schedule, those are the three priorities I work with.

Business Planners and Calendars

In an effort to keep track of all this, I have tried perhaps a dozen different sizes and styles of planners but have never been wholly satisfied with any. I've used pocket-size and desk-size planning systems from a variety of publishers. For a couple of years, I used a Cambridge planner, consisting of a 7-by-9-inch three-ring binder with assorted calendars and dividers. I customized it to fit my business needs, which included adding a set of alphabetical index-tab dividers that enabled me to turn quickly to lists, schedules, and notes. For some reason, though, when I was ready to order refills several years ago, Quill had stopped carrying Cambridge products, and I couldn't find what I needed locally. Fortunately, a good friend and colleague of mine gave me a Franklin Quest planner/calendar for Christmas, and it proved outstanding in many respects.

You probably won't find a planner/calendar that's perfect for you and your business in every way. One secret to making a planner/calendar work well is to customize it to fit your specific needs.

The best advice I can offer you is to consider your needs and go shopping. You'll find planners and systems of every shape, size, and purpose at office-supply outlets and many department stores, and through some mail-order sources. There is even planner/calendar software available for people who are never far from their computers or who carry portable computers with them. You'll also find software that works in conjunction with conventional planners. If you can't find the ideal planner/calendar, create your own.

Some people like to keep a separate business diary; I don't. My planner is a record of most of my business dealings and transactions, assignments, appointments, meetings, phone calls, correspondence, and more. I see no reason to duplicate any of this. Consequently, I do not discard my various to-do lists and schedules. For years I have saved and filed them as a record of my business. I suggest you do likewise, or keep a business diary if you prefer.

Make Your Own Planner/Calendar

When you eventually grow weary of searching for the perfect planner while using the inferior or inappropriate designs of others, perhaps you'll do as I did not long ago and create your own.

I used my computer to design standard 8½-by-11-inch planner pages, then ran them through a three-hole punch so that they would fit into a large, zippered ring binder that keeps everything handy and organized. As I use up a month's worth of pages, I file them in a standard 1-inch binder that holds a year's worth of documents as a permanent record of my business activities.

I have planner pages for listing and scheduling business and other activities by the day, week, month, and quarter, which I'll share with you. You can use them as they are or as idea sources for designing pages that better accommodate your business and personal life.

You'll notice that I have three different designs for the daily planner pages. The first one is for the busiest people who need a full page per day to keep track of all they must do. I assigned this one the filename "Awful Day Plan."

The person whose business day is merely hectic and complex might prefer the set with the filename "Complex Day Plan," which requires four pages per week. The format is identical for the Monday/Tuesday, Wednesday/Thursday, and Friday/Saturday pages. The left column of the fourth page lays out Sunday the same as other days, but the right column provides space for journal entries and reminders for the coming week.

The simplest of my daily planners has the filename "Simple Day Plan." This one lays

Monday: _____ / _____

APPOINTMENTS/MEETINGS:

1. _____
2. _____
3. _____
4. _____
5. _____

MUST DO (Priority 1):

1. _____
2. _____
3. _____
4. _____
5. _____
6. _____
7. _____
8. _____
9. _____
10. _____
11. _____
12. _____

SHOULD DO (Priority 2): _____

1. _____
2. _____
3. _____
4. _____
5. _____
6. _____
7. _____
8. _____
9. _____
10. _____

TRY TO DO (Priority 3): _____

1. _____
2. _____
3. _____
4. _____
5. _____
6. _____
7. _____
8. _____

PHONE/E-MAIL/LETTERS:

1. _____
2. _____
3. _____
4. _____
5. _____
6. _____
7. _____
8. _____
9. _____
10. _____
11. _____
12. _____
13. _____
14. _____

NOTES/REMINDERS:

_____
_____
_____
_____
_____
_____
_____

JOURNAL:

_____
_____
_____
_____
_____
_____
_____
_____
_____
_____
_____
_____
_____
_____
_____
_____
_____

Filename: Awful Day Plan

Monday: _____ / _____

NOTES: _____

_____

_____

_____

_____

_____

APPOINTMENTS/MEETINGS:

_____

_____

_____

_____

_____

PHONE/E-MAIL/CORRESPONDENCE:

_____

_____

_____

_____

_____

_____

_____

MUST DO TODAY (Priority 1):

_____

_____

_____

_____

_____

_____

_____

_____

_____

SHOULD DO TODAY (Priority 2):

_____

_____

_____

_____

_____

_____

_____

Tuesday: _____ / _____

NOTES: _____

_____

_____

_____

_____

_____

APPOINTMENTS/MEETINGS:

_____

_____

_____

_____

_____

PHONE/E-MAIL/CORRESPONDENCE:

_____

_____

_____

_____

_____

_____

_____

MUST DO TODAY (Priority 1):

_____

_____

_____

_____

_____

_____

_____

_____

_____

SHOULD DO TODAY (Priority 2):

_____

_____

_____

_____

_____

Monday: _____ / _____

NOTES: _____

_____

_____

_____

_____

_____

TO DO TODAY:

1. _____
2. _____
3. _____
4. _____
5. _____
6. _____
7. _____
8. _____
9. _____
10. _____
11. _____
12. _____

Tuesday: _____ / _____

NOTES: _____

_____

_____

_____

_____

_____

TO DO TODAY:

1. _____
2. _____
3. _____
4. _____
5. _____
6. _____
7. _____
8. _____
9. _____
10. _____
11. _____
12. _____

Wednesday: _____ / _____

NOTES: _____

_____

_____

_____

_____

_____

TO DO TODAY:

1. _____
2. _____
3. _____
4. _____
5. _____
6. _____
7. _____
8. _____
9. _____
10. _____
11. _____
12. _____

Thursday: _____ / _____

NOTES: _____

_____

_____

_____

_____

_____

TO DO TODAY:

1. _____
2. _____
3. _____
4. _____
5. _____
6. _____
7. _____
8. _____
9. _____
10. _____
11. _____
12. _____

Friday: _____ / _____

NOTES: _____

_____

_____

_____

_____

_____

TO DO TODAY:

1. _____
2. _____
3. _____
4. _____
5. _____
6. _____
7. _____
8. _____
9. _____
10. _____
11. _____
12. _____

Saturday: _____ / _____

NOTES: _____

_____

_____

_____

_____

_____

TO DO TODAY:

1. _____
2. _____
3. _____
4. _____
5. _____
6. _____
7. _____
8. _____
9. _____
10. _____
11. _____
12. _____

Sunday: _____ / _____

NOTES: _____

_____

_____

_____

_____

_____

TO DO TODAY:

1. _____
2. _____
3. _____
4. _____
5. _____
6. _____
7. _____
8. _____
9. _____
10. _____
11. _____
12. _____

JOURNAL:

_____

_____

_____

_____

_____

_____

_____

_____

_____

NEXT WEEK:

_____

_____

_____

_____

_____

_____

_____

Filename: Simple Day Plan

Week: _____ / _____ / _____

APPOINTMENTS/MEETINGS:

_____
_____
_____
_____
_____

NOTES/REMINDERS:

_____
_____
_____
_____
_____

CRAFTS:

1. _____
2. _____
3. _____
4. _____
5. _____
6. _____
7. _____
8. _____
9. _____
10. _____
11. _____
12. _____
13. _____
14. _____
15. _____
16. _____
17. _____
18. _____
19. _____
20. _____
21. _____
22. _____

PHONE/E-MAIL/LETTERS:

1. _____
2. _____
3. _____
4. _____
5. _____
6. _____
7. _____
8. _____
9. _____
10. _____
11. _____
12. _____
13. _____
14. _____
15. _____

CHORES:

1. _____
2. _____
3. _____
4. _____
5. _____
6. _____
7. _____
8. _____
9. _____
10. _____
11. _____
12. _____
13. _____
14. _____
15. _____
16. _____

TOP PRIORITY/MUST DO:

1. _____
2. _____
3. _____
4. _____
5. _____
6. _____
7. _____
8. _____
9. _____
10. _____

January

APPOINTMENTS/MEETINGS:

_____
_____
_____
_____
_____
_____
_____
_____

TOP PRIORITY/MUST DO:

_____
_____
_____
_____
_____
_____
_____
_____

CRAFTS:

_____
_____
_____
_____
_____
_____
_____
_____
_____
_____
_____
_____
_____
_____
_____
_____
_____
_____
_____
_____
_____
_____
_____
_____
_____
_____
_____

BUSINESS/HOUSEHOLD CHORES:

_____
_____
_____
_____
_____
_____
_____
_____
_____
_____
_____
_____
_____
_____
_____
_____
_____
_____
_____
_____
_____
_____
_____
_____
_____

First Quarter

JANUARY PROJECTS:

_____
_____
_____
_____
_____
_____
_____
_____
_____
_____
_____

FEBRUARY PROJECTS:

_____
_____
_____
_____
_____
_____
_____
_____
_____
_____

MARCH PROJECTS:

_____
_____
_____
_____
_____
_____
_____
_____
_____
_____
_____

HOUSEHOLD PROJECTS:

_____
_____
_____
_____
_____
_____
_____
_____
_____
_____

DEADLINES:

_____
_____
_____
_____
_____
_____
_____
_____
_____
_____
_____

REMINDERS:

_____
_____
_____
_____
_____
_____
_____
_____
_____

out the entire week in two pages, with room left on the second page for journal entries and reminders. Although this may be the simplest of all three designs, it is deceptively so. This is not a planner for people who don't have much to do; it's the one for people who have plenty to do but have their lives under control.

If you need the page-a-day planner, as I once did, I suggest you spend time examining your business to find ways to streamline it. The idea here is to eventually get your life organized enough for you to use the four-page-a-week planner. Then keep working at it until the simple two-page-a-week version is all you need. I've reached a point where I'm using the Simple Day Plan and actually leaving some lines blank most days.

The daily planner is for getting down to specifics. The weekly planner can be a bit more general; nevertheless, it shows some specific items—such as appointments, meetings, and correspondence—that just get transferred to the daily planner in a timely fashion.

The monthly planner is broader yet. It requires one page per month, and each page is identical to the others.

Quarterly planners are for listing and scheduling major projects and keeping track of more distant deadlines and income due. The four pages required are identical except for the month names.

Keep watch for ways to customize these pages to suit your needs. On the daily planner pages, for example, you might want to dedicate some space to certain activities you repeat daily or regularly. If you walk, run, or ride a bike for fitness, you might wish to record your daily mileage. Perhaps you're dieting and want to count calories. Or you might want to keep track of the time you spend working out on exercise equipment.

Design other pages to further specialize and customize your planner. You can also add alphabetical, monthly, and other index tabs; page finders; printed calendars; plastic pocket pages; business-card holders; and other items you'll find in the Quill catalog and at local office-supply outlets.

Business Files

Every business in America is confronted with the management of a tremendous amount of paperwork that gets more unwieldy every year. I'm not exaggerating when I tell you that this paperwork load can be overwhelming and if left unchecked will soon bury you. If you've worked in industry or government, you already know how bad the situation can be.

When I worked in the jet-engine industry, it was common knowledge that for every ton of engines and spare parts we built, we generated two tons of paperwork.

As a self-employed entrepreneur, you will be able to exercise some control over the paperwork snarl, but don't expect total success. To give you an idea of how severe the problem is, my local post office receives eight bags of mail for every bag it sends out, which means that on the average, postal patrons in my community get eight times as much mail as they generate. In my case the ratio is even more lopsided—probably about twenty pounds received for every pound I send out.

If you haven't given much thought to managing this paper mountain, you had better do so immediately. The best time to set up the systems you will need is now. If you wait until paperwork is stacked in teetering piles, sorting and filing will be worse chores than they already are.

Think of all this business paperwork as a vast and disorderly herd of cattle, with just enough wild and rangy longhorns mixed in to create the potential for stampedes. As range boss, your job is to keep this unruly bunch of critters headed in the right direction.

Your goal is to get every piece of essential paper into its proper place—a file in which other similar papers are kept. What's most frustrating, though, is that the paperwork you deal with is a mass of miscellany. Directing each piece from a general pile to a specific file is among the most tedious of tasks. The process can be streamlined and vastly improved.

An Efficient Interim Filing System

Set up an interim filing system that will corral groups of related documents. Use the same principle to move paper through your entire business process until it eventually ends up in neatly and conveniently stored file folders.

In the good old days, before we wasted so much paper, a typical business manager was able to maintain reasonable control with the aid of the cubbyholes in a rolltop desk and three file trays. The life of the business manager, however, has become far too complicated to be organized with three baskets labeled *In, Out,* and *Pending*.

You'll find a number of products available for performing these yeoman duties, such as desktop sorters and organizers, literature sorters, and all sorts of stacking trays and baskets.

Commercially available desktop organizers—available in metal, plastic, or wood—are freestanding units that can add the efficiency of the old rolltop desk to any modern desk or worktable. They come in various sizes and capacities, but all are limited in their usefulness mainly to keeping desktops uncluttered.

Literature organizers resemble bookcases, with numerous cubbyholes designed for routing and holding standard letter-size documents and publications. They're usually made of metal, corrugated board, or both. Some are modular stacking units that you can add to as your needs dictate. They come in sizes ranging from six to seventy-two compartments.

One stacking tray or basket will hold about as much paperwork as one compartment of a literature organizer. A system of trays probably costs slightly more than a literature organizer of comparable capacity, but trays have the advantage of versatility; they fit practically anywhere, and the system easily expands by one or a dozen units at a time.

When my home-based business was a part-time venture, I got by fine with a system that consisted of a dozen trays. As my business has grown and expanded into many different areas, the system has had to grow with it and now consists of seventy-six trays.

I'm not going to list all the subject labels, but I will tell you how I've labeled some of these trays to keep paper organized and moving. Standing in my office, between a four-drawer filing cabinet and some bookshelves, is a stack of seventeen trays that handle all my highest-priority paperwork and most of what accumulates in my daily mail. Among them are trays labeled *Priority 1*, for anything requiring action within seven days, and *Priority 2*, for action within thirty days. Seven trays are for specifically routed correspondence, and one is labeled *Miscellaneous Correspondence*. The *Order* tray holds paperwork for products, literature, and anything else I need to order during the month. The tray labeled *File* is for anything I've acted on that is now ready for routing to a specific file tray and ultimately to a folder in a filing cabinet. The top tray in the stack holds my outgoing mail until my next trip to the post office.

Despite the tonnage of catalogs you receive regularly, I'll bet you can never quickly find the one you're looking for. Murphy must have a law about that. Solve your problem, as I did, with stacking trays. Eleven of the trays in my studio keep all my catalogs orderly and readily at hand.

Among the most active trays are those that function as follow-up files. Other busy trays include *Accounts Payable, Accounts Receivable,* and *Business Taxes.*

I make my tray labels with self-adhesive plastic embossing tape and one of those little Dymo label makers. If you use plastic stacking trays, you may find that embossed-tape labels don't stick as well as they should and eventually come off. Here's a tip: Wrap a cloth or paper towel around your finger, dampen it with cigarette-lighter fluid, and wipe the surface where you plan to affix the label. By the time you peel the backing off the label, the surface will be dry and ready, and the label will stay on. If you ever need to change a label on a tray, lighter fluid will also remove any gummy residue left by the old label.

An interim filing system is easy to maintain and serves several valuable purposes. First, it lets you sort and route paperwork quickly and efficiently. When you need something that has not yet made it to a file folder, it's far easier to sort through the paperwork in one file tray than to waste untold amounts of time pawing through stacks of miscellaneous magazines, articles, catalogs, and other accumulated paperwork. By far the greatest value of my interim system is that it keeps me from being buried in paperwork while allowing me to put off the actual job of filing until the last second.

An Active Filing System

I have also worked to make my active files easier to use and maintain. Over a period of about two years, I gradually converted all my file drawers to hanging files. (In case you're not familiar with them, hanging-file systems consist of inexpensive metal racks from which specially made folders are suspended. Also, some filing cabinets are made specifically for hanging files.)

The racks are easy to assemble and install in any filing cabinet or desk file drawer. In my system, I use standard and box-bottom (large-capacity) hanging file folders to hold all the materials I keep in manila file folders. The advantage of a hanging system is that file folders stand upright and are easily removed and returned without other folders falling over.

In recent years I have also color-coded many of my active files with self-adhesive file-folder labels made for such purposes. This makes it a lot easier to locate a particular file folder in any stack of folders I'm currently working with. Every folder in the files for this book, for example, has a folder-tab label with a narrow orange stripe across the top.

You'll find such labels available in perhaps two dozen colors at most office-supply outlets. Colored file folders offer another way to color-code your filing system.

Computer Files

Computers offer users a convenient way to reduce much of the paperwork shuffling by filing material electronically. Although I doubt that computer storage will soon be able to replace conventional filing systems entirely, it can help streamline the filing process and certainly promises to be even more usable and versatile in the future.

It took me a while to get used to the advantages of computer filing, and I still catch myself now and then making a hard copy of a letter or other document, when digitized documents are more easily stored and retrieved and don't require the multiple handling most paper documents do.

Another tremendous advantage of digital storage is that it takes up so little space as compared with conventional paper storage. What I have stored on diskettes and compact discs in four small cabinets would probably fill several four-drawer filing cabinets and many feet of bookshelves.

Dead Files

Filing cabinets are expensive. Corrugated filing boxes are cheap. Use filing cabinets for all your important active files. Use corrugated filing boxes for dead files—those that aren't active but must be retained for one reason or another. Tax files for previous years, for example, can go into a dead file instead of taking up valuable space in a cabinet. You'll certainly find other files you must keep but don't use very often that would be better routed to a dead file.

Quill Corporation and other office suppliers sell boxes for this purpose. As you fill each box, label it clearly with a felt marker and store it in any dry storage area.

Problems in Managing Your Business

No business runs so perfectly or smoothly that there's never a problem, but the manager who works to anticipate problems is usually able to sidestep the worst ones and keep on course with a minimum of hassles and hardships.

Identifying Problems

What kinds of problems might the home-based craft professional have to face? Every aspect of your business can be problematic. You can have problems with vendors, customers, and other people. Your business vehicle, craft machinery, and office equipment can give you trouble. You can have financial, legal, and operational difficulties. You can have insurance problems, tax troubles, and minor irritations or major worries over bookkeeping, paper shuffling, phone service, time management, printing, plumbing, electricity, the neighbor's cat, termites, and door-to-door peddlers.

The potential seems boundless, but the right attitude and strategy can keep catastrophes contained. Understand that running a business is mainly a matter of encountering, identifying, and solving problems, big and small. Most of what we've covered so far in this book has to do with managing minor problems and avoiding major ones.

Don't Needlessly Complicate Matters

A problem is any matter, concern, or situation that poses an obstacle or causes some degree of difficulty or perplexity in the carrying out of a task. It's as simple as that. Too many people, however, make too big a deal out of problem solving. If you can think, you can make decisions. If you can make decisions, you can solve problems. If you can solve problems, you can run a successful business.

In recent years I've read a number of reports and articles written by business consultants and other authorities. I have watched some of these experts in action and have grown especially wary of business gurus who turn decision-making and problem-solving processes into complex and convoluted exercises. If I followed all their silly suggestions, I'd never get anything done.

There's also a tendency among business consultants and academics to complicate otherwise simple processes with highfalutin terminology. With the possible exceptions of sociology and literary criticism, no other discipline is more encumbered with buzzwords, catchphrases, jargon, and invented terms.

It's always best to anticipate problems so that you can avoid them or deal with them comfortably and effectively. Like life, however, business is full of surprises. If you're smart, you'll take them in stride and learn from them.

I'm frequently reminded of the old medical joke in which the physician asks the patient what the problem is. The patient raises an arm and says, "It hurts when I do this." The doctor responds, "Then don't do that."

How many times have I made some foolish move and instantly regretted it? Pardon me while I count. Invariably, I think to myself or even say aloud, "I won't do that again." Live and learn.

Productivity

Productivity is the essence of your business, so you will have to keep track of it, manage for it, and improve it in any way you can.

Analyzing Productivity

Many businesses, especially the larger ones, use reports to analyze and manage productivity. Although managers often custom-design reports for specific purposes, some of the more generic reports contain information that allows experienced managers to track productivity.

Profit-and-loss (P&L) and cash-flow reports are two you can use to analyze your productivity, but they won't prove valuable until after you've been in business a while. Your first year, you will be working with P&L and cash-flow *projections*, which are useless in measuring actual production. Even in your second year, you might not find these reports of great value. It takes some practice and experience to be able to scan the columns and translate the numbers into productivity measurements.

The Production/Sales/Income Report

Meanwhile, you may want to design a report that does a better job for you. For a number of years, I used a document I called a Production/Sales/Income (PSI) report, which I prepared monthly. This is a simple report that is easy to compile. It covers gross sales and income but does not include information about expenses and other costs of doing business.

For the person unaccustomed to using P&L and cash-flow reports, however, this is a good alternative.

I stopped using these reports for several years and instead relied solely on P&L and cash-flow figures, which provide a more accurate picture of net income and profits. I reasoned that this was not only better information, but data available to me anyway, which made the PSI reports seem redundant. I've since reinstated my PSI reports, however, for the very simple reason that I like them. I'm willing to devote the little time required for the gain derived. PSI reports are a good exercise, they provide a different perspective, and they are valuable micromanagement tools. The reports tell me when I've done a good job and when I haven't—useful praise and prodding.

In conjunction with this report, I use PSI worksheets, which I keep in the same binder as my business planner and calendar. These are four loose-leaf pages identified at the top as *Production, Sales, Assignments/Commissions,* and *Income.* Each evening after work I log in dates, descriptions, and amounts on the proper worksheets, which I then use on the last day of the month to prepare my PSI report.

On the left side of the report, under the heading *Production,* I list the description of each job completed, the market for which it was produced, and the date of completion. If I'm producing for inventory, I note that as well. On the right side of the page, I list the actual or estimated value of each job. I do the same under the headings *Sales, Assignments/ Commissions,* and *Income.* I total the amounts for each category and use that information in the summary section at the end of the report.

After I enter the information and figures for the month's income, I run a line across the page and put my summary under it. For example, under the heading *September Summary,* I list Accounts Receivable as of September 1, September Production, September Sales, September Assignments/Commissions, September Income, Accounts Receivable as of September 30, and Year-to-Date Income as of September 30. A quick glance at my summary lets me know where I stand and where I need to concentrate my efforts.

The information under any heading might be artificially inflated or deflated for one reason or another. For example, in looking back through some of my old reports, I found one for March showing I landed assignments worth $15,600—two $300 assignments and one for $15,000. What's not shown in the raw data, however, is how that income trickled in during the subsequent months.

Production/Sales/Income Report—September

	Actual Value or Estimated Value
Production	
1. Inventory: 800' NaturWud molding—9/7	$800.00
2. Valley Cutlery: 20 small cutlery blocks—9/14	570.00
3. Valley Cutlery: 20 large cutlery blocks—9/21	770.00
4. Inventory: 600' RufCut molding—9/23	600.00
5. Coast Museum: matting & framing—9/27	1,100.00
6. Oak 'n' More: assorted oak products—9/30	1,650.00
September Production	**$5,490.00**
Sales	
1. Bay Arts Festival—9/4-5	$1,826.50
2. Riverfront Mall: misc. wood products—9/10	647.86
3. Sand & Sun Festival—9/18-19	2,185.75
4. Bayway Wood Products: frame molding—9/22	550.00
5. Woodcrafter's Gallery: misc. wood products—9/27	762.19
6. Frame-It Shop: frame molding—9/30	300.00
September Sales	**$6,272.30**
Assignments/Commissions	
1. PNW Tug & Barge: custom framing—9/24	$1,500.00
2. *Crafter's Journal:* "Making Moldings"—9/29	500.00
September Assignments/Commissions	**$2,000.00**
Income	
1. Bay Arts Festival—9/4–5	$1,826.50
2. Enchanted Forest Gift Shop—9/9	438.78
3. Sand & Sun Festival—9/18-19	2,185.75
4. Hanford Press—9/30	4,169.23
September Income	**$8,620.26**

September Summary	
Accounts Receivable as of September 1	$ 3,494.78
September Production	$ 5,490.00
September Sales	$ 6,272.30
September Assignments/Commissions	$ 2,000.00
September Income	$ 8,620.26
Accounts Receivable as of September 30	$ 7,350.05
Year-to-Date Income as of September 30	**$50,482.03**

Some months, production figures can come out extremely low, even as low as $0.00, but without reflecting actual production. It's a matter of how the game is played. I established the rules, which I work and live by. Although I might spend much or even all of a month working on a major project, or several, if I don't finish by month's end, it doesn't get logged in or credited to that month's production. Figures for some later month, then, will end up being artificially inflated, just as this month's figures were deflated.

Figures for sales and income can fluctuate broadly at times but should be relatively stable over the course of a year. The idea is to work to gradually increase both to a comfortable level that provides you with good income and a schedule you can live with.

To make the system work, you need to set production and income goals at the beginning of the year. Come up with a reasonable monthly figure and work hard to meet it. As a part-timer, you might establish $1,000 or $1,500 as your monthly PSI goal—less or more, depending on your situation. As a full-timer, you might need to make $3,000 to $4,000 or more each month. When you exceed your PSI monthly goal, it feels good, and you can give yourself a pat on the back. When you fall short of your goal, do the same, but make the pat a kick, and aim a little lower on the torso.

If you own a computer or plan to buy one for your business, you may wish to set up a PSI-report system on a disk, as I may do when time permits. Instead of logging information onto worksheets each evening, I will eliminate the worksheets altogether and enter the pertinent information directly onto a disk each morning, after I check my e-mail messages. I'll then print out a report at the end of the month. I think such a streamlined system will require less than an hour's work a month but will provide a wealth of useful information.

Production Control

If there's a secret to success in any business—large or small, corporate conglomerate or sole proprietorship—it's production control. Any business manager who ignores or fails to understand the importance of production control is headed for disaster.

Of course, every product-oriented business depends to some extent on ideas, designs, and creative thinking. But without careful control of the production processes that ensure timely manufacture and delivery of top-quality products at the lowest possible cost, the creative processes are futile exercises. If creativity is the heart of your business, production control is the central nervous system.

The job of production control comprises five phases or steps:

1. *Analyzing production needs.* Once you have created a workable and salable design, you must determine its manufacturing requirements. What materials will you need to acquire? What tools are required; will you need to buy any? How does production of this product affect the production of other products? Will you be making all the components, or can you buy some ready-made parts?

2. *Planning the production process.* Product parts must be acquired, made, or modified, then put together. What is the proper sequence of acquisition and assembly? How is the product to be finished? Should some parts be painted, varnished, or otherwise finished before assembly? How many different tool setups are required? All of this must fit into a working production plan.

3. *Implementing the production plan.* Make sure essential materials, supplies, and parts are conveniently and safely contained and readily accessible near the production area. Have all required tools nearby. Make sure machinery is set up for the first production phase and, if possible, any subsequent phases. Keep the production plan handy for later tool setups.

4. *Streamlining production.* During initial production, remain alert for operations that can be accomplished more safely, quickly, and efficiently. Watch for any possible production alterations that could save time, money, or both. Set production goals at the outset, and try to exceed them as you proceed. Analyze all operations during and after production and take careful notes on ways to improve any phase. To save on tool setup time, watch for production phases that are compatible with other products in your line.

5. *Conducting micro cost analysis.* Macro cost analysis is important as a way of letting you know how your business is doing overall and how it can be improved. Micro cost analysis of each product and each part of each product will give you a much better picture of where your production strengths and weaknesses are and where and how you can improve production to reduce costs or make your operations more cost effective.

For most products, machine setup is the most time-consuming and costly part of production. When coming up with a prototype of any design, I usually spend more time on machine setup and organization than I do on actual assembly and finishing. So as I develop my production plan, I look for opportunities to batch-process and try to implement them wherever possible.

A word of warning is in order, however. Although batch processing of components reduces costly setup time, it can lead to monotony and result in safety hazards, especially when power tools are used. So part of your production plan should include some relief steps that will help alleviate boredom and keep you alert.

Let's say you have 300 identical parts to cut with a table saw, and you know it will take about an hour to complete this step. After about twenty minutes the job's going to get monotonous, and your concentration will waver as your mind drifts. At this point it could be dangerous to continue cutting, but it would be silly to stop after cutting 100 parts and set up for the next cutting step, only to have to return to those remaining 200 parts and retool twice more for them.

It's better to include steps that will relieve monotony while maintaining an efficient production schedule. For example, if the parts you're cutting will need light sanding before assembly, you can spend twenty minutes cutting 100 parts and then move to the sander, where that relief step might take ten minutes. Return to the saw for the next twenty minutes and sand for ten more. One more cycle, and you'll be finished cutting and sanding 300 parts—and will have done so in safety.

Batch finishing—staining, painting, varnishing, stenciling, texturing, weathering, antiquing, and such—also saves time and promotes efficiency. It's also possible to gang-finish quantities of several different products at once.

Improving Production

Although production control is mainly associated with manufacture, it's also inextricably tied to planning and to marketing. There are more ways of improving production than simply increasing output or directly reducing costs. So solving production problems often means examining production plans at one end and marketing strategies at the other.

Production Case Study

Perhaps the best way to illustrate how all this works is with an actual case study of one of my products and how I've gone about improving production and reducing costs to increase profits and broaden my market base. This story has no end, because production control is an ongoing process for any product that remains in production as part of a product line.

Over the years I've designed several mug trees that have proved popular. One design began as a way of using scraps of maple left from the manufacture of butcher blocks, cutting boards, and other items I make. Eventually, though, it became a first-line product for which I purchase maple instead of using only scraps.

As with most products, my mug tree has certain advantages and disadvantages as compared with competing models. Although I occasionally see other hardwood mug trees made of maple or oak, most that show up at craft fairs and gift shops in coastal Oregon are made of California laurel, which is widely promoted and marketed in the Pacific Northwest as Oregon myrtle or myrtlewood. The wood itself is beautiful, and all the myrtlewood hype is difficult to compete with. Most of the myrtlewood mug trees I've seen, though, are primitively designed and unrefined and hold only four mugs. My maple mug tree is of much better design and manufacture and holds six mugs.

The trunk of my tree is of thicker stock, and all edges are decoratively routed. The bases of my trees are also routed to provide a more finished appearance. Competing myrtlewood trees usually have just the edges of their trunks and bases rounded over by sanding. Retail prices on the myrtlewood trees, and similarly designed and manufactured oak and maple trees, typically range from $18.50 to $22.50.

My original production plan allowed me to compete with those prices at craft shows and anywhere else I'm able to sell directly to the customer. But my costs were too high to permit wholesale pricing to retail outlets, such as gift shops.

Here's a breakdown of my original micro cost analysis:

Maple Mug Tree
I. Materials

A.	Mug pegs (31.5 cents x 6)	$1.89
B.	Maple trunk	1.17
C.	Maple base	.67
D.	Stain and lacquer	.50
E.	2" x #8 screw	.03
F.	Glue (this is a guess)	.10
G.	¼-inch felt dots (2.4 cents x 4 = 9.6 cents)	.10

Material Costs $4.46

II. Labor
    A. $10/hour
    B. Time per unit = 30 minutes

Labor Costs $5.00

III. Overhead
    A. $5.00 x 33.3%

Overhead $1.67
Manufacturing Costs $11.13

IV. Profit
    A. $11.13 x 100%

Profit $11.13
Price $22.26

As you can see, my cost studies indicated that I could manufacture my maple mug trees and competitively market them at a price of $22.25 each, or even a bit higher. These trees will readily sell for any price under $30. If I wholesaled them at $22.25, however, the retail markup would take them to a prohibitive $44.50.

I examined my production plan, eliminated a couple of minor logjams, set a new production goal of four units per hour, and was able to reduce my manufacturing costs dramatically. Here's the breakdown:

Maple Mug Tree II
(Improved Labor)

I.	Materials	$ 4.46
II.	Labor (15 minutes per unit)	$ 2.50
III.	Overhead ($4.46 x 33.3%)	<u>$ 1.49</u>
IV.	Manufacturing costs	$ 8.45
V.	Profit	<u>$ 8.45</u>
VI.	Price	$16.90

The good news is that I was able to reduce manufacturing costs by increasing productivity, and although my "paper" profits are reduced in my study, my real profits increase if I continue selling the mug trees at craft shows for $22.25 each. My real profit in the original production plan was the difference between my manufacturing cost of $11.13 and my selling price of $22.25, or $11.12 per unit. In my improved plan, the actual profit is the difference between my manufacturing cost of $8.45 and my selling price of $22.25, or $13.80: a profit increase of $2.68 per unit.

The bad news is that $16.90 is still too high as a wholesale price. This tree will not sell at $33.80, or what would more likely turn out to be $33.88 or $33.95.

I'm not about to give up on the idea of getting my mug trees into retail outlets. Western maple has been one of the most economical domestic hardwoods available to me. Myrtlewood is the most expensive, but it carries that highly publicized, yet mythical, native-Oregon mystique that makes it ideal for the manufacture of gift items and Oregon souvenirs.

Alder is another native hardwood that has been ignored for years in America but is widely used elsewhere as a fine-furniture wood. In Pacific Northwest logging operations, alder has been treated as trash: something to be burned as slash, cut up for firewood, or chipped for particle board. Recently, though, it has begun to get some of the attention it deserves as a useful and beautiful hardwood. An alder mill has opened a few miles from where I live, and I think I can significantly trim my manufacturing costs by using alder instead of maple in my mug trees.

Here's how my micro cost analysis works out, based on my improved productivity and a reduction of material costs from $4.46 to an estimated $3.54 per unit:

Alder Mug Tree
(Improved Labor and Materials)

I.	Materials	$ 3.54
II.	Labor	$ 2.50
III.	Overhead ($3.54 x 33.3%)	$ 1.18
IV.	Manufacturing costs	$ 7.22
V.	Profit	$ 7.22
VI.	Wholesale price	$14.44
VII.	Retail price	$28.88

Voilà! The magic figure—under $30. This mug tree will sell at a retail price of $28.88, which will allow me to wholesale it profitably. My profit margin won't be as great as it is for the mug trees I sell directly, but this will expand my market base in an important way, help to spread my sales evenly over a twelve-month period, and put my products in gift shops during the busy tourist season.

I will also test-market the alder units with the maple units at the craft fairs. If I find that alder trees move as well as the maple ones, I might discontinue the maple mug trees and work exclusively with alder, thereby increasing my direct-sale profits even further.

It doesn't stop there. I believe that production control is an ongoing process. I'm already planning other tests that might trim my manufacturing costs even more. For example, alder is a closer match than maple with the birch mug-tree pegs I use. So I think I'll be able to eliminate the stain I'm currently using and simply apply a polyurethane or lacquer finish, which could eventually cut my finishing costs in half.

Ready-Made Components

Another important part of your production plan is determining whether to make all the necessary parts for any product or buy ready-made components when they're available. Of course, cost is the primary determinant in this decision, but remember, time is money. Even though you might save a good bit by manufacturing any component, you could end up spending more time than the saving justifies.

When I began making my mug trees, I showed one to a friend and fellow craftsman. He dutifully admired it and then said, "I didn't know you had a lathe." When I acknowledged that I didn't, he was astonished that I was actually paying good money for ready-made mug-tree pegs when I could turn my own for about half the price.

Well, to make my own pegs, I'd have to invest several hundred dollars in a lathe, which is only a minor deterrent, inasmuch as I could put the tool to good use on other products. Even if I had a lathe, though, I still couldn't make the pegs as cheaply as I can buy them ready to use.

In my early cost analysis for the same project, I looked at the possibility of making my own square felt cushions from ¼-inch-wide felt tape. By buying the tape in 900-foot rolls, I could hold my felt costs to about 3 cents per unit. But I would also have to cut four squares per unit, which may not seem like much labor, until you imagine cutting 200 squares for fifty mug trees. I decided to spend a dime a unit for ¼-inch felt dots instead.

What's important is that you consider the feasibility and cost efficiency of using ready-made parts wherever you can. Determine what it costs *in cash* and *labor* to make the component yourself and what it costs to buy the finished component.

Business Communication

Many small-business operators fail to fully appreciate how important written and oral communications are to every business, regardless of its size, product, or service. From the onset, you must be prepared to handle all communication professionally and to document all aspects of your business.

Letterhead and Business Cards

Your first order of business should be to design an attractive letterhead and have stationery, envelopes, and business cards printed. You can design a logo or find suitable clip art you can combine with an attractive typeface. If you're no good at this sort of thing, seek help. Some printers can assist with logo design, but not all are skilled at it. You might want to enlist the aid of a graphic artist to provide original art or work with you to come up with a good design. You'll also find useful information and ideas in the book *How to Design Trademarks and Logos* by John Murphy and Michael Rowe.

Try to make your logo simple, uncluttered, and attractive. If possible, avoid artwork that might date the design. You will use your logo often and become associated with it. For that reason, you shouldn't change it unless absolutely necessary, and then make as few modifications as possible.

When you've come up with a design, you'll have to decide what color paper you want, what quality, what color of ink, and what type of printing. Use good-quality, twenty-pound or heavier bond paper and avoid heavily textured surfaces. Go with white or cream or a pleasantly muted shade of gray, beige, blue, or green. Stationery, envelopes, and business cards should be the same color.

Ink color should contrast or coordinate with paper color. Just make sure the ink is dark, the paper light. Some common combinations are black ink on white paper, black on gray, dark brown on cream, dark brown on beige, dark blue on light blue, and dark green on light green. You can also pick two or three contrasting colors of ink, but that will increase your costs.

You'll have a choice between raised and flat printing. Raised type has a sharper, classier look, but it's usually more expensive than flat printing and might not be done locally. If you use a computer with a laser printer, order flat printing for stationery and envelopes. Pick whatever suits you for business cards.

You will probably want to use your logo on your various printed forms, such as invoices, work orders, sales slips, and statements. It will cost you extra, but the price shouldn't be prohibitive.

Document Your Transactions

Get into the habit of documenting all your business transactions in some way. This doesn't mean you have to write down everything you do in narrative form, although you sometimes should. Every time you write up a work order or prepare an invoice, you are documenting a transaction, so keep copies for your files. Also make a copy of every business letter you write; it can be a carbon copy, carbonless copy, photocopy, or computer copy.

What about documenting phone calls? You have several options. If you keep a business diary, you can log your phone calls there. Some businesses maintain phone diaries for documenting all telephone communications. As I mentioned earlier, I don't keep a business diary; nor do I keep a phone diary. I let my planner system document my day-to-day operations. When I need to take important notes, I use ruled yellow pads I buy by the dozen; then I date the notes and route them to their proper files. I keep one of these pads near each of my telephones so that I can take notes on important conversations. I date and file them as I do other notes.

Why all the documentation? It keeps you from relying on what might prove to be an unreliable memory. It helps you get jobs done the way customers want them done. It provides dated references for any necessary follow-up or other action. It also protects you and your business in a variety of ways and can be used as evidence in a court of law.

Be Prompt and Courteous

Promptness is the mark of a professional; courtesy is the mark of a person who is pleasing to deal with. So in all your communications, be prompt and courteous. See to all business correspondence in a timely fashion and return phone calls within twenty-four hours if possible.

Follow-Up

Follow-up is essential and should be timely, but don't make it any more complicated than it needs to be. I often hear colleagues talk about keeping follow-up logs for all their projects and correspondence. They list everything they send out, the date sent, destination, and other information they deem essential. I don't do any of that, yet I have a follow-up system that will rival any in efficiency. It's part of the interim filing system I wrote about earlier in this chapter.

Everything in my business has a paperwork connection. My invoices and statements are carbonless two-part forms—original to the customer, copy for my files. When I write a query, proposal, or business letter, I keep a copy. The job of follow-up is a simple matter of going to the appropriate trays in my interim filing system at the end of each month and examining the contents for anything that requires attention.

I send statements to any clients who haven't paid their bills that month. I then attach a copy of each statement to any pertinent paperwork, such as work orders and invoice copies, and return it to the Accounts Receivable tray. Any account still unpaid thirty days later gets a late charge added to that month's statement.

I don't have to do a tremendous amount of follow-up. In fact, with my receivables, it's usually a matter of just pulling all the copies of invoices, statements, and such as they're paid. There are usually only a few left at the end of a month, and some months there's nothing left in the tray except that month's new billing.

I have considered turning all this over to my computer, but I haven't been able to devise a cost-effective computer billing and follow-up system that's as simple as my manual system.

Procrastination

As you can see, I put this section off until last. Despite all the words of warning in the various guides for small-business operators and home-based entrepreneurs, procrastination is not the damning malady we're led to believe. Actually, I think most of us are procrastinators by nature. In fact, I'm not sure I could trust (or believe) anyone who claims never to have procrastinated. The trick is to avoid giving in to the urge too often and never to jeopardize a deadline simply because you didn't feel like doing a job.

Few chronic procrastinators end up running their own businesses. Anyone who's that prone to putting things off is also apt to put off starting a business.

Anyone with brains enough to get up in the morning knows you can't constantly put jobs off and expect your business to succeed. There will be days when you just don't feel like working or doing jobs you hate; I assure you of that. But you'll get the work done anyway, because that's your job, and you're a professional. The success of your business depends on those simple facts.

Should you worry about procrastination? I think you can put that off for now.

Chapter Ten

Marketing Your Craft Business

Although marketing and selling are inextricably interrelated, selling is but one part of the marketing process. Selling is the exchange of merchandise for cash; marketing encompasses all aspects of the transfer of goods from manufacturer to consumer. A sound marketing program includes promotion, public relations, and customer service, as well as the storage, sales, and shipment of products.

Marketing is your ultimate purpose and should be part of every phase of your business. It precedes the manufacture and transcends the sale of merchandise. First, last, and always, your business is marketing.

Creating a Marketable Reputation

The magnitude of the marketing effort surprises many fledgling entrepreneurs. It's a big and important job that takes a lot of time and effort, especially in the beginning. Much of it amounts to researching and finding potential customers, then building a sound and salable reputation. During the early stages of your business, all this might consume more than half your time.

When I started my business as a part-timer, I wasn't wholly prepared for the task and for how my time would be divided. I was naive enough to think I could spend countless hours creating masterpieces, then devote any time left to the more mundane matters of managing a business and marketing my work. In short, I saw these chores as spare-time tasks.

After a severe attack of reality, I realized I was spending about 80 percent of my time managing and marketing my business and 20 percent in creative pursuits. Meanwhile, though, I was also establishing a marketable reputation that would eventually enable me to improve that ratio.

No matter what sort of craft(s) you're engaged in, your most important product is professionalism. You must establish a reputation for reliability, competence, punctuality, courtesy, superior services, sacred deadlines, and guaranteed satisfaction.

Market Analysis

As a home-based entrepreneur, you can't afford to conduct surveys and market analysis the way major corporations do, but you should develop a solid notion of who and where your customers are and what they're looking for.

The problem is, too many artisans get it backward. They manufacture products first, then try to find buyers for them. It must be the other way around: Research the marketplace; then develop products that will sell there.

In the home-based craft business, the key to successful market analysis is observation. You must pay close attention to how and where craft products are sold, what prices other artisans charge for their products, and who buys them.

Find the Right Outlets

In order to determine who will buy your products, you must first decide where your best sales outlets exist. Here are some possibilities:

- Gift and souvenir shops
- Arts-and-crafts galleries
- Specialty shops
- Chain stores
- Craft malls
- Mail-order outlets

- Arts-and-crafts co-ops
- Aquarium and museum gift shops
- Craft fairs
- Wholesale trade shows
- Retail trade shows
- Festivals and bazaars
- Sidewalk arts-and-crafts exhibits
- Farmers' markets
- Flea markets and swap meets
- Powwows and potlatches
- Vendor carts and booths
- Food and beverage festivals
- Open houses and craft parties
- The World Wide Web

Start Small and Market Locally

Learn about every possible nearby outlet. Determine what's available in your town, in your county, and within easy driving distance of your home. Find out where and when all the craft fairs and related exhibits are in your community and in nearby towns. Similarly, identify and locate all the shops and galleries that might handle your products. These should be your primary marketing targets.

Gradually extend your research to include potential sales outlets throughout your state and region. Take some scouting trips and check out all the shops and galleries.

In every town you visit, your first stop should be the local chamber of commerce or visitor center. Collect general descriptive literature about the community and find out about all the local events that offer opportunities for craft sales. Most chambers and visitor centers have brochures and other publications that provide all the details you need. Be sure to get literature about shopping, restaurants, and lodging, and ask for a complimentary copy of the local phone directory. Back home, file this material for later reference and trip planning.

Tell the person at the visitor center what you're up to and ask for recommendations. Sometimes potential outlets exist in the least likely places.

On Oregon's north coast, for example, is the small town of Tillamook, in a sparsely populated county of the same name. Since shortly after pioneer settlement, this has been dairy country. In fact, the county is home to about 24,000 people and 40,000 cows. At the north end of town, on the main highway, is a large industrial-looking building and a sign over it that reads TILLAMOOK CREAMERY ASSOCIATION. It's known locally as "the cheese factory" and would seem a more likely place to find Kraft products than craft products.

Nevertheless, about half the complex is devoted to tourist facilities, including a restaurant, deli, soda fountain, and wine shop. Nearly a million tourists stop here each year and take the popular tour of the cheese factory. They emerge from the industrial end of the complex into a large sales area, where they can buy all kinds of cheese products as well as books, gifts, and craft items. It's the second-largest man-made tourist attraction on the Oregon coast and a tremendous sales outlet for artisans with the right products.

During your scouting trips you'll learn about many other places you might not normally consider to be possible sales outlets. In my travels, I've found gift shops and galleries at hotels, motels, and lodges. I've been surprised to find artworks and craft items on sale at a good many restaurants, marinas, and even campgrounds and RV parks.

Make the most of your trips. Ask the locals lots of questions. Take copious notes. And observe, observe, observe.

Selling to Shops and Galleries

When I started in business as a part-time entrepreneur, I sold my work through a gallery in Fairbanks called The Alaska House. In those days the standard shop or gallery markup was 50 percent of wholesale or 33.3 percent of retail, meaning that two-thirds of the retail price was my share and one-third went to the shop or gallery. So if I sold a product for $10 or $100, it got marked up to $15 or $150 (or usually $14.95 or $149.50).

Now the markup is 100 percent of wholesale, or at least it is where I live. That means shop and gallery owners simply double the wholesale price and keep half for themselves. Some markups are even higher, particularly if the artisan has underpriced the products.

A couple of years ago, my next-door neighbor began making resin castings of his wood carvings to sell through gift shops. He figured $19.95 would be a good retail price for his cast whales, so he wholesaled them at $10 each. I tried to tell him he was underpricing his work, but he was reluctant to charge more, until I returned from one of my trips to report that I'd found his resin whales on sale for $39.95—a 300 percent markup.

The time to approach shop and gallery owners is not when customers are standing in line to pay for their purchases. Plan your scouting trips for the off-season, if possible, so that you can talk to proprietors at their leisure. Ask them about the possibility of selling your work through them and find out when they normally do their buying.

If you're not familiar with local customs and don't know when the buying and selling seasons are, ask other local artists and artisans.

Where I live, summer is a big selling season. Store buyers generally order stock from late winter to late spring, but some shop and gallery owners set aside only a few weeks to buy for the coming season. The owners of one of my favorite galleries do all their budgeting in January and buy all their stock in February. The artist or artisan who shows up in March hoping to sell to these folks is out of luck.

September and October are usually busy buying times for shop and gallery buyers stocking for the coming holiday season. After Christmas things are pretty slow where I live. Elsewhere—in the Southwest or deep South, for example—tourism is at its peak at that time. So you'll have to find out on your own what the seasons are in your part of the country. If you plan to travel and sell outside your region, take the climatic differences into account.

Craft Fairs and Trade Shows

Craft fairs are often held at shopping malls, armories, high-school gymnasiums, community centers, and other facilities that provide adequate display space and parking. Some are juried and require potential exhibitors to submit samples of their work to a committee that determines whether the products are of sufficient quality. Others let space to anyone who can come up with the fees.

Local craft fairs are great places for artisans new to the business to get involved with a minimal investment. Some fairs, especially those in the larger metropolitan areas, are excellent sales outlets for neophytes and veterans alike.

Fees for the smaller local weekend fairs usually range from $25 to $125. Promoters of the big shows on the national circuit can demand $200 to $500 or more and have no problem filling spaces.

Retail trade shows are usually held in coliseums, stadiums, convention centers, fairgrounds, and other places that have the capacity to hold large crowds. They're open to the public and are thematic in nature. Craft professionals interested in exhibiting at these big shows need to match their products with the show themes and should expect to pay from $300 to as much as $1,500 in exhibit fees.

Wholesale trade shows are closed to the public. This is where manufacturers' reps, business owners, professional buyers, industry media, and others gather for big-time marketing. These shows can be huge, as was the one I attended several summers ago at Chicago's McCormick Place, where there were 10 square miles of exhibits displaying the products of 3,000 companies. Of all the shows, these are the least likely to be of value to home-based craft professionals.

Susan Ratliff has written a dandy little book for persons interested in knowing more about craft fairs and trade shows. It's called *How to Be a Weekend Entrepreneur: Making Money at Craft Fairs and Trade Shows*. I happily recommend it.

Dress for Success

Keep in mind that you're selling yourself as well as your products. Whether you're calling on a shop owner or staffing a booth at a craft fair, dress for success. That doesn't necessarily mean you must look like a Fortune 500 CEO, but you ought to present the appearance of a successful professional. Demonstrate that you have good taste and judgment by dressing well for the occasion in clothes of good quality.

Appearance isn't everything, but it can make a big difference to some of the people to whom you hope to sell your products. Scruffy attire can imply sloppy craftsmanship and careless business practices. A good appearance, on the other hand, has never cost anyone a sale.

Hiring a Rep

Some craft professionals don't need or want the services of sales representatives; others swear they can't get by without them. You'll have to decide for yourself. If you detest dealing directly with shop and gallery owners, or if you would rather spend most of your time on the creative aspects of your business and leave the sales to someone else, you're a good candidate for a rep.

Sales reps can be indispensable for artisans who want to place their work nationally. Reps who attend the big shows can write a lot of orders, so if you're aspiring toward a high level of production, consider representation.

Reps function as independent contractors and are paid a percentage of the sales they make for you—usually 10 to 15 percent. Some also charge for show expenses.

You'll be expected to sign an agency agreement or contract, which you may want your attorney to review. Remember that contracts should be mutually beneficial to both parties and that much of what appears in any such agreement ought to be negotiable.

Ask local craft professionals whether they're represented, and if so, what they think of their reps. That's one way to find a rep to handle your work. Another way is to ask proprietors of gift shops and art galleries for recommendations.

Publicity and Promotion

Publicity is one kind of advertising money can't buy. Advertising is a concentrated and focused effort that you pay for and exercise some control over. Although you can and should guide publicity and control it as best you can, you might not have the final word here; someone else probably will.

Publicity has the same goal as advertising—to get your business known and recognized by potential clients or customers—but is accomplished in different ways. Good publicity is far more valuable than advertising for the very reason that it *isn't* paid for. Consequently, it seems more like an unsolicited endorsement, which it often is.

It's important to get your name before the public at every opportunity. As with advertising, the greatest effects of publicity are cumulative, so it's equally important to keep your name and business image prominent and visible to potential customers.

Organizations

A number of organizations can assist you in a variety of ways. National professional and business associations can offer helpful hints and provide a useful exchange of ideas.

Association with your peers across the nation can lead to important business contacts.

Local business, fraternal, and other organizations can also do much to publicize and promote your business and put you in touch with people you need to know: likely customers or business associates. I met and got to know both my attorney and my insurance agent when the three of us worked as committee members for a local chapter of a national conservation organization. I also made other significant contacts through the same association. Donating my time and work to the organization got my business a good bit of publicity as well.

Some associations worth investigating are your local chamber of commerce, Jaycees, Junior League, Lion's Club, Rotary, and Kiwanis. And don't overlook the special-interest clubs and associations, some of which are listed in the "Source Directory" at the back of this book.

Media Publicity

A little media publicity can go a long way toward getting your name and business reputation known in your community. What's more, capturing local media attention might be a lot easier than you think.

Newspapers of all sizes run business profiles and features on local entrepreneurs. Small-town and suburban weeklies are the surest bets, but dailies also use such stories.

Visit the newspaper offices in your area, and talk to the appropriate business editor, features editor, managing editor, or whoever assigns such stories. Keep in mind that it's best to have an angle or "peg" for the story.

Perhaps you have an interest or specialty that will add appeal to a story about your business. Do you use any unusual techniques, materials, or equipment in your craft business? If you use any locally manufactured or regionally indigenous natural materials, that can be of particular interest. Do you work with traditional materials and ancient processes? Is there a local historical peg to your business and its story? At the other end of the spectrum, perhaps you work with the latest high-tech equipment to create products for the twenty-first century.

Local radio and television stations often air interview and talk shows that can prove good sources of publicity. TV stations might even want to film your products, or perhaps show you at work creating your crafts. Don't miss an opportunity like that.

Public Relations

Another way to exploit print and electronic media is with public-relations (PR) techniques. For instance, you can use news releases to get the word out about you and your business, but you should have a good news peg to make your release irresistible.

News releases differ from the kind of publicity discussed earlier in that you furnish the copy to the media. You generate the story, either by writing it yourself or hiring someone to write it.

There's nothing wrong with writing your own news releases, providing you possess the necessary skills. If you can't tell a semicolon from a semiconductor, however, get help.

Some editors will use your releases with little or no modification. Others might follow up with phone calls to augment the material you furnish. Still others might assign a reporter and photographer to do a feature or photo spread.

Even if there's nothing particularly unusual or exciting about your business, you can still use public relations to your advantage. Special events, awards, and honors are always good news pegs. So when you win "best of show" at a juried exhibition or take three blue ribbons at the county fair, make sure your local print- and electronic-media people know about it. When a professional association elects you to high office or presents you with an award, get out a news release.

News Release Format

News releases should follow a standard format that includes all pertinent information. You can use plain white paper or your letterhead. You might want to design a news release form that incorporates your logo.

Make sure your business name, address, and phone number appear prominently at the top of the page. The words *News Release* should also appear in large boldface type near the top of the page. Also include the current date, release date, length, and the name and phone number of the person to contact for further information.

For releases going to print media, provide the length, expressed as an approximate number of words. It's best to keep releases brief—usually no more than 200 to 300 words, never more than 500.

NEWS RELEASE

Crafts Unlimited
1492 Columbus Drive
Moon Valley, IN 54321
(123) 555–4545

To: _____   Date: _____

_____   Length: _____

Release Date : _____   Contact: Terry Johnson,
                                                 Owner/Manager

Title, Headline, or Topic

(more)

Releases for the electronic media should be shorter yet, with length expressed in seconds. You'll have to read them aloud at a normal broadcast pace and time them. Try to confine them to thirty seconds. You can also provide several versions of the same release running different lengths—say, twenty, thirty, and forty seconds. The recipient can then pick whichever one fits an available time slot.

The release date can be the same as the date you prepared and mailed the release, or some later date, tied to an event. Your release might have a limited life or time span, which you should indicate on the release-date line. For example, if the release should run only during the month of July, the release date should be July 1 through July 31.

Below the information lines, immediately preceding the text of the release, center a title, headline, or description of contents.

If a release requires more than one page, all pages except the first should be numbered sequentially and should carry an abbreviated title at the top. At the bottom of every page except the last, enclose the word *more* inside parentheses. At the end of the text, two spaces beneath the final paragraph, center the words *The End* or the symbol # # #.

Use simple sentences and short paragraphs. Avoid jargon and technical language. Use what's known as the *inverse pyramid style,* in which you attempt to put all the essential information into the first paragraph or two and the least important material toward the end. That way, an editor can trim it from the end to accommodate space limitations.

Remember the five *W*s and the *H*—Who, What, Where, When, Why, and How—and make sure every release answers each of those questions.

Displays and Donations

The more people who see your work, the greater the cumulative effect, and the better the likelihood that potential customers will think of you when special needs arise. You must take advantage of every opportunity to publicize your craft and business.

Showing Your Work

The obvious places to show craftwork are galleries and museums, but there are other places you shouldn't overlook. Of course, you should try to sell your work to galleries, and you should enter your handicrafts in exhibit competitions. Talk to gallery owners about handling your work and museum curators about sponsoring one-person shows.

Any business or institution with a lobby, great hall, waiting room, or reception area is a potential client or displayer: banks, clinics, hospitals, dental offices, law offices, executive offices, nursing homes, retirement facilities, senior centers, restaurants, hotels, motels, bed-and-breakfast inns, resorts, ski shops, dive shops, and so on.

You should be able to sell a variety of craftworks to these and other establishments. Those who aren't interested in buying often can be persuaded to display a selection of handicrafts in exchange for their decorative value. Others might agree to display and sell your work on consignment.

In my community, a number of banks display original artwork, photography, and handicrafts as a way of helping artists and artisans get their work before the public. One retirement complex regularly sponsors and publicizes art, craft, and photographic exhibits. Restaurants and resorts up and down the West Coast similarly display the works of local artists, photographers, and artisans.

Donating Your Work

Donating craft items to fund-raisers can also net you some promotional rewards. When a local nonprofit organization sponsors a fund-raising dinner, auction, or sale, the press is sure to cover the event, and you can share the promotional value when you are listed as one of the donors to the cause.

Volunteering Your Time and Skills

Volunteering is another way to reap the rewards of publicity. You can volunteer your time and energies for events sponsored by local nonprofit organizations. The organizations will be grateful for your help, and local media will no doubt help publicize the events, both before and after.

If you can teach what you know about crafts, offer to teach a one-day or weekend craft workshop through a local organization, college, or university. Such a workshop will call for advance publicity in the form of newspaper articles and public-service announcements on radio and television.

Advertising Your Business

Whether or not you need to advertise depends largely on the kinds of crafts you're engaged in and the way you normally sell your products. Once you've decided or been advised to advertise, you must determine the best, most cost-effective medium or media.

Should You Hire an Agency?

Advertising is expensive, and advertising agencies are more expensive yet. A good agency can do much for the business ready to use its services but can prove too costly for the new entrepreneur.

A better plan for the start-up home-based craft business is a program that relies primarily on self-promotion, publicity, public relations, and limited advertising. There are media staff people who will work with you on creating ads, and you can do much of the work yourself. First, you must determine what advertising avenues are available in your community or working area, then which will serve you best.

Advertising Media

Advertising takes many shapes and shows up in a variety of places, from the covers of matchbooks to the sides of buses. The media that craft professionals most commonly use include the Yellow Pages, newspapers, magazines, radio, television, brochures, direct mail, and specialty advertising. Costs vary widely, as does effectiveness, and each form has its advantages and disadvantages.

- **Yellow Pages.** This is one of the most basic forms of advertising. It can amount to a simple listing or an elaborate display ad. Staff is available to help you with layout.
  Advantages: Directories are widely distributed to everyone who has a phone. People who use the Yellow Pages are in the market for services or products. Directories are kept on hand for a year.
  Disadvantages: This is a passive medium, meaning that people can freely choose what ads to read or ignore. Deadline lead times are long. It's seldom a good idea to include price information.

- **Newspapers.** The larger the newspaper's circulation, the greater the potential effect of its advertising, but also the higher its advertising rates will be. Nevertheless, newspapers remain among the most used media for localized advertising.

  Advantages: Newspapers have a high degree of reader acceptance. Ads are available in a great variety of sizes and can be clipped and saved. They can include as much detail and information as you want or can afford.

  Disadvantages: Newspaper ads are relatively expensive. Newspapers are a passive medium and are short-lived (soon discarded). Poor reproduction is a problem at many small newspapers, which will do injustice to any photographs you include with your ads.

- **Magazines.** Under the right circumstances, magazine advertising can be effective for certain craft businesses. Rates are high, often prohibitive, even in some city and regional magazines.

  Advantages: Reproduction is usually superior to that of other print media. Target marketing is most precise. You can include as much detail as you wish, and ads can be clipped and saved.

  Disadvantages: Magazines usually have long lead times for deadlines. Like other print media, they are passive and are often so cluttered with ads that readers skip them.

- **Radio.** In some places radio is the best medium for small-business advertising. What's more, radio usually offers competitive rates and ready markets.

  Advantages: Radio provides a good way to target a specific group. Commercials can reach a high percentage of the target group. It's an active medium—commercials are hard to avoid or ignore.

  Disadvantages: Large metropolitan areas are cluttered with many stations, which tends to fragment the audience. Commercials must be short, usually with limited details. There's no way to show what products look like. The most effective time slots can be prohibitively expensive.

- **Television.** Generally, television is the most effective advertising medium, but also the most expensive. The proliferation of cable companies has made cable advertising more competitive and has put TV advertising within the reach of many small businesses. For some craft businesses, it holds promise.

Advantages: Cable TV is a good medium for reaching specific market segments. A single TV commercial can reach a large audience. Television is a fairly active medium, though less so than it previously was because of the current widespread use of VCRs, DVDs, and remote control. Television also offers an unlimited range of special effects.

Disadvantages: Production costs are high, as are the costs of purchasing commercial time. Audiences have been greatly fragmented by the proliferation of cable channels. The best time slots are either taken by national advertisers or are too expensive for small businesses.

- **Brochures.** For many crafts, brochures can be an effective form of advertising.

  Advantages: Brochures provide the greatest amount of space for detailed information. They offer the opportunity to showcase your creative skills and can function as a portfolio of your work. You can use brochures to reach a targeted direct-mail market. Brochures are fairly easy to create and can be relatively inexpensive to produce.

  Disadvantages: Brochures can be time consuming and expensive to distribute. Those with color photography are expensive to produce.

- **Direct Mail.** Advertising by mail can cost dearly in money and time, but with the right client list and selective mailing, it can be a valuable marketing tool.

  Advantages: Direct-mail campaigns can reach a broad or concentrated market, depending on your needs and approach. This is also an ideal way to distribute brochures to your target markets and to encourage repeat business.

  Disadvantages: Response rates are often low. Postal rates and printing costs continue to rise to levels that are often prohibitive.

- **Specialty Advertising.** This category includes all the promotional paraphernalia such as pens, pencils, letter openers, digital clocks, calendars, buttons, caps, and other products bearing a business logo and advertising message. Most of these gimmicks probably have greater goodwill value than advertising worth.

  Advantages: Nobody objects to getting these little freebies. You can target your market, and the advertising value lasts as long as the object.

  Disadvantages: Space for advertising is usually very limited. You must buy a large quantity to keep the per-item cost down. Effective distribution can be costly and time consuming.

Tips on Advertising Effectively

Media staff and your local Small Business Development Center can offer helpful hints for getting the most out of your advertising dollar. Meanwhile, here are a few more tips that should help:

- Make sure all your print ads prominently display your name, address, and phone number.
- When advertising via radio, remember that listeners might be on the road and unable to write down your phone number. Refer them to your Yellow Pages ad instead of giving your phone number.
- The greatest effect of advertising is cumulative. It's better to buy several small ads or commercials than a single large one.
- Radio commercials are most effective when tied in to simultaneous print ads.
- Don't make your ads and commercials too busy; keep them concise and uncluttered.
- Saturday is usually a poor day to advertise in newspapers; Sunday is a good day.
- A good way to make newspaper ads last longer is to buy space in a weekend supplement or weekly TV and entertainment guide or section.
- The best times for radio commercials are the morning and evening driving slots, usually from 6:00 to 9:00 A.M. and from 3:00 to 7:00 P.M.
- Cut costs on direct-mail advertising by designing brochures and flyers to be self-mailers.

The Best Advertising of All

The best advertising is the kind you can't buy. It grows out of your reputation and is spread by people who know your work and freely recommend it. It's often called *word-of-mouth advertising,* a term that leaves the impression that this is a form of exposure that is usually narrow in scope. In practice, however, it's a wonderfully compounding dividend that you collect on the principal of your good reputation.

Internet Marketing

During the 1990s the Internet grew into a huge and powerful marketing venue for businesses large and small. For a couple of years in the mid-1990s, the World Wide Web reportedly doubled in size about every three to four months. Since then, annual growth rates have run from about 70 to 150 percent. According to Media Metrix, Inc., an Internet tracking company, consumer on-line sales reached $78 billion in 2002. If you're not sure exactly how your home-based business may fit into the Internet marketing scheme, however, welcome to a large and growing club whose membership includes yours truly.

Without question, every home-based business proprietor should own a computer with full Internet access. E-mail alone makes the small monthly charge for Internet services worthwhile. Add to that the ability to conduct all sorts of research and find every imaginable kind of information on the Internet—twenty-four hours a day, seven days a week—and access becomes essential.

Nevertheless, access to and presence on the Internet are two distinctly different matters, the latter requiring a good bit more thought, consideration, planning, and money than the former. Many small businesses, like most of their corporate big brothers, can profit dramatically by selling products and services on the World Wide Web. Even some home-based craft businesses can benefit from establishing and maintaining their own Web sites, but the Web is certainly not the ideal marketplace for everyone. Whether the Internet is or may be a good sales tool for you and your business is a matter you must settle for yourself after careful study. Two good places to begin your research are your favorite book outlet and the Internet itself.

Doing the Research

Books are always good sources of information on any subject, but the Internet changes constantly and rapidly, often making books on Internet topics obsolete within a year or two. Consequently, only the most current books about computers and the Internet are worth reading. Considering the short shelf life of books about computers and the Internet, I've become reluctant to recommend specific titles. My best advice is to look for books or revised editions published within the last two years—the more recent the better.

At this writing, a good book to start with is *Marketing on the Internet* by Jan Zimmerman and Hoon Meng Ong. You might also check out *Essential Business Tactics for the Net* by Larry Chase. These books cover all the essentials and options, as well as the practical and technical aspects of developing your own Web presence. Should you wish to consider the Internet as a potential medium for advertising your business, check out *Advertising on the Internet* by Robbin Zeff and Brad Aronson.

If your local bookstore doesn't stock these titles, ask to order them; it's always good to support your local businesses. Should you meet with any resistance, however, point your Web browser at www.amazon.com or www.barnesandnoble.com, and order them on-line.

To search craft topics on the Internet and find out how other craft businesses and companies are using cyberspace to market their wares and communicate with their clientele, conduct your own Web searches using any of the search engines and search topics covered in Chapter 8. Then, at your leisure, visit the many craft Web sites listed in the "Source Directory" at the back of this book.

Determining the Web's Worth

In general, if your business depends mainly on local clients and in-person transactions, the Internet probably won't be of much value as a sales tool. On the other hand, if you can mass-produce handcrafted products with widespread appeal, far-flung markets, and competitive prices, as well as provide quick and convenient delivery by mail or parcel service, then perhaps the Internet would be a good sales outlet for your business.

What about the rest of us: the busy picture framer with plenty of local customers and more than enough business, the peripatetic crafter who makes an enjoyable and comfortable living traveling the craft-show circuit, the needlecraft artisan whose profitable business is just the right size, the master woodworker who got into this business in the first place to get away from all the hustle and hype, the metalsmith who already has a hard time keeping local stores supplied, the burly chainsaw sculptor who needs a crane and a forklift just to move his big bears and totem poles, and all the other people who are just too busy running their home-based craft businesses to be bothered with learning about and spending more money on yet another technological advancement? Is the World Wide Web the right place for our businesses? Can we profit from Internet presence? The only answer to these questions is a definite maybe: maybe now, maybe not, maybe never, or maybe in the near or distant future.

Developing and Maintaining a Web Site

Those entertaining the prospects of developing and maintaining a Web site should realize that they will probably need help. As the authors of *Marketing on the Internet* put it: "Developing a Web site can be daunting. Leonardo da Vinci was probably the only person who could have done it all himself—from stunning graphic design to elegant code, from mastering the aesthetic vocabulary of six different media to computing bandwidth requirements." Unless you're a computer nerd and a Web wizard, you'll need to hire the services of a Web-site designer.

Web-page design is a relatively new profession, having grown up with the World Wide Web since 1993, so many designers are still learning and developing their skills. Moreover, the mere fact that someone has hung out a "Web Designer" shingle doesn't necessarily guarantee proficiency in the practice. By visiting an assortment of Web sites, you'll soon discern that not all Web designers are created equal. Some are skilled programmers who have no eye for pleasing layouts. Others are creative artists who might not possess the technical skills to keep a Web site functioning flawlessly, day in and day out. The best are computer experts with a thorough grasp of the necessary hardware and software, a flair for graphical and typographical treatments, and a track record that bears out their expertise on all fronts.

To find and interview promising prospects, start in the Yellow Pages of your local telephone directory, under such headings as "Computer Dealers," "Internet Marketing Services," and "Internet Service Providers." If you live in a rural area or small town, check the directories of the nearest big cities. Ask for recommendations at your local Small Business Development Center and at the computer science department of any nearby community college or university. You can also search the World Wide Web for prospective designers by using various search engines and the key phrase *web page design.*

Investing Money and Time

Web site costs vary tremendously depending on the locale and the size and configurations of the site under consideration. Setting up a site can cost from a few hundred dollars for the simplest catalog of up to five pages, to a few thousand dollars for a multipage interactive site with shopping, credit card, and e-mail support. A competent designer should be able to provide accurate estimates of all charges associated with planning, building, and maintaining your Web site, including the costs of domain registration, hardware and software, Web page setup and maintenance, ISP setup and maintenance, disk-space rental, Web advertising, and of course the designer's fees, which will probably run from $50 to $150 an hour.

Time is another important consideration, and time, in any business, always equates to money. Time is also an aspect of Web-site development and maintenance that too many business managers ignore. Peter Kolonia summed it up in the April 1998 issue of *Popular Photography:* "Be forewarned, though, the major investment in creating a Web site isn't money or skill, but time. The difference between a ho-hum site and an invigorating one that keeps visitors coming back, is the hours spent in creating, maintaining, and renewing it. It requires a real commitment. . . ."

But then, what aspect of any home-based business doesn't?

Visiting Existing Sites

Whether you are serious about planning, developing, and implementing a Web site in the near future or are merely considering the possibilities and examing your options, spend some time visiting and studying the various sites that function as on-line brochures or craft catalogs, as well as the interactive sites that serve as sales outlets for craft supplies and other products. You'll discover many by conducting searches using the criteria listed under "101 Craft Search Topics" in Chapter 8.

Developing New Products, Services, and Markets

Eventually, your business will probably grow to a point of saturation, either yours or the markets'. When that happens, you may or may not wish to keep expanding. If you're comfortable with the size of your business and income, you can reduce your marketing effort to maintaining the status quo and replacing markets that fall by the wayside. By then your reputation might even be such that your business won't need much publicity, promotion, or advertising.

During your business's formative years, or possibly for the life of your business, you'll need to be concerned with continued growth and increased profits. If you are managing wisely and getting as much as possible out of every dollar you earn and spend, you will need to turn your attention to developing new products and markets as ways of increasing income and profits.

I've been running my own business for more than twenty-five years, and I still remain alert for new marketing opportunities. I keep a list of markets I haven't yet cracked but would like to. I then try to develop one or several new markets or upgrade existing ones each year.

Identify Your Opportunities

No matter what kinds of products you create and sell, you'll discover other products and services you can provide and a great number and variety of potential new markets. Before you venture into new areas, though, you need to consider carefully the kinds of work that interest you, the kinds that don't, and those that are of marginal interest. You need to identify and analyze the markets as well. And it's equally important to know and understand your limitations.

I enjoy working at several crafts, and there are a number of others that are intriguing enough for me to try my hand at. Some, however, don't interest me in the least, and others require more technical or artistic expertise than I possess. Certain crafts require only a minimal investment in tools and machinery or are compatible with the equipment I already own. Others require equipment I consider prohibitively expensive or for which I cannot justify the investment.

It's important to keep all such considerations in mind when you think about expanding your business and developing new markets.

The Show Must Go On—and On, and On, and On . . .

During tight financial times some marketing outlets go out of business, which can leave you high and dry if they represent a substantial part of your income—especially if you don't have alternative markets to fall back on.

I have learned from such experiences that I must continually strive to develop new markets and improve my existing ones, but too often I have so much work that I don't have time for that crucial part of my operation. All I can do then is promise myself I will do better when the pressure is off.

Toward that end, I make only one New Year's resolution and repeat it every January 1. I have it printed in bold black on an index card pinned to the bulletin board above my computer desk. It reads simply: WORK SMARTER THIS YEAR!

A Dozen Ways to Expand Your Craft Business

1. *Represent other artists and artisans.* If you enjoy calling on shops, galleries, and other sales outlets, consider becoming a sales rep for other arts-and-crafts professionals in your region. You can continue selling your own products and earn commissions on the works of others.

2. *Start an arts-and-crafts co-op.* Get the names and addresses of other artists and crafts professionals in your community and nearby vicinity. Schedule a meeting and invite them all to attend. Then discuss the prospects of forming a local co-op. You can then rent a building where you can set up stalls for each participating exhibitor. Members can take turns staffing the cash register. With a dozen members, your turn will come up only once every twelve business days.

3. *Organize and promote arts-and-crafts exhibits.* Meet with mall managers, city officials, and others in charge of renting building space, including community buildings and armories, and find out what it costs to rent exhibit space for a weekend. Then organize arts-and-crafts exhibits and rent space to exhibitors. You manage and advertise the event and earn a profit for your trouble.

4. *Sell your designs or patterns.* If you've come up with some popular and highly salable designs for craft items, have your designs, working plans, or patterns offset-printed. Then sell them to crafts hobbyists and other crafts professionals. You can sell them directly at craft fairs, through craft magazines, and on the Internet.

5. *Publish an artsy-craftsy newsletter.* If you own a computer and word-processing or desktop-publishing software and have some writing and editing ability, consider publishing a newsletter and selling subscriptions to hobbyists and professionals interested in crafts.

6. *Write and sell craft how-to articles.* Put your writing ability and word processor to work producing articles that describe and illustrate how to make various craft items. If you're an expert artisan but a mediocre-to-terrible writer, collaborate with a professional writer and split the profits.

7. *Write and sell craft how-to books.* If you can write and sell craft articles, you can write and sell craft books. If your ideas and designs are good enough but your writing's not, find an interested writer to collaborate with you.

8. *Sell arts-and-crafts supplies.* Find wholesale sources for the arts-and-crafts supplies that sell best to hobbyists and professionals and stock them for resale. You can sell them at craft fairs and from your home.

9. *Add related craft items to your line.* If your business has settled into a holding pattern, give it a jolt by adding related craft items to the line you now produce. You probably already have all the necessary tools on hand and many of the essential materials.

10. *Add unrelated craft items to your line.* Learning a new craft can be time consuming, but it can also prove to be highly profitable. Unrelated craft items added to an already successful line will provide variety and broaden your market base.

11. *Start a direct-mail business.* Get busy photographing your line; then put a brochure or catalog together. Buy targeted mailing lists and bulk-mail your promotional material to prospective direct-mail buyers. Don't overlook the possibility of selling craft materials and supplies as well as finished craft items.

12. *Put your computer to work.* Your computer can help you broaden your market base and increase your profits in a variety of ways. Buy inexpensive calligraphy software and offer that service as part of your business. Buy software for horoscopes and news of the past; then take your computer on the road with you and sell horoscopes and special "this day in history" birthday and anniversary greetings at craft fairs, swap meets, and flea markets.

Selected Bibliography

Attard, Janet. *The Home Office and Small Business Answer Book.* 2nd ed. New York: Owl Books, 2000.

Bealer, Alex. *The Successful Craftsman: Making Your Craft Your Business.* Barre, Mass.: Barre Publishing, 1975.

Blum, Laurie. *Free Money for Small Businesses and Entrepreneurs.* 4th ed. New York: John Wiley & Sons, 1995.

Boyd, Margaret A. *Crafts Supply Source Book.* 5th ed. Cincinnati: Betterway Books, 1999.

Chase, Larry. *Essential Business Tactics for the Net.* 2nd ed. New York: John Wiley & Sons, 2001.

Covington, Michael A., et al. *Dictionary of Computer and Internet Terms.* 7th ed. Hauppage, N.Y.: Barron's, 2000.

Dible, Donald, ed. *What Everybody Should Know about Patents, Trademarks and Copyrights.* Reston, N.J.: Prentice-Hall, 1982.

Duboff, Leonard D. *The Law in Plain English for Craftspeople.* 3rd ed. Loveland, Colo.: Interweave Press, 1993.

Foster, Frank H., and Robert L. Shook. *Patents, Copyrights, and Trademarks.* 2nd ed. New York: John Wiley & Sons, 1993.

Gumpert, David E. *How to Really Start Your Own Business.* 4th ed. Needham, Mass.: Lauson Publishing Co., 2003.

H&R Block, Inc. *H&R Block Income Tax Guide.* New York: Collier Books, published annually.

Harper, Stephen C. *The McGraw-Hill Guide to Starting Your Own Business: A Step-by-Step Blueprint for the First-Time Entrepreneur.* New York: McGraw-Hill, 1992.

Hart, Russell. *Photographing Your Artwork.* 2nd ed. Buffalo, N.Y.: Amherst Media, 2000.

Herring, Jerry, and Mark Fulton. *The Art & Business of Creative Self-Promotion.* New York: Watson-Guptill Publications, 1987.

Hornung, Clarence P. *Treasury of American Design.* New York: Abradale Press, 1997.

J. K. Lasser Institute. *J. K. Lasser's Your Income Tax Guide.* New York: Prentice-Hall, published annually.

Long, Steve and Cindy. *You Can Make Money from Your Arts and Crafts: The Arts and Crafts Marketing Book.* Scotts Valley, Calif.: Mark, 1988.

Meltzer, Steve. *Photographing Your Craftwork: A Hands-on Guide for Craftspeople.* 2nd ed. Loveland, Colo.: Interweave Press, 1993.

Palder, Edward L. *The Catalog of Catalogs VI.* Bethesda, Md.: Woodbine House, 1999.

Pfaffenberg, Bryan. *Webster's New World Dictionary of Computer Terms.* 9th ed. New York: Simon & Schuster, 2001.

Pressman, David. *Patent It Yourself.* 9th ed. Berkeley: Nolo Press, 2002.

Ratliff, Susan. *How to Be a Weekend Entrepreneur: Making Money at Craft Fairs and Trade Shows.* Phoenix: Marketing Methods Press, 1991.

Rose, Grace Berne. *The Illustrated Encyclopedia of Crafts and How to Master Them.* Garden City, N.Y.: Doubleday & Company, 1978.

Zechlin, Ruth. *Complete Book of Handcrafts.* Newton Centre, Mass.: Charles T. Brandford Company, 1967.

Zeff, Robbin, and Brad Aronson. *Advertising on the Internet.* 2nd ed. New York: John Wiley & Sons, 1999.

Zimmerman, Jan, and Hoon Meng Ong. *Marketing on the Internet.* 6th ed. Gulf Breeze, Fla.: Maximum Press, 2002.

Source Directory

Associations

American Association of Home Based Businesses
P.O. Box 10023
Rockville, MD 20849
Phone: (800) 447–9710
Fax: (301) 963–7042
E-mail: aahbb@crosslink.net
Web: www.aahbb.org

American Craft Council
72 Spring Street
New York, NY 10012
Phone: (212) 274–0630
Fax: (212) 274–0650
Web: www.craftcouncil.org

The Arts & Crafts Society
1194 Bandera Drive
Ann Arbor, MI 48103
Phone: (734) 358–6882
Fax: (734) 661–2683
E-mail: info@arts-crafts.com
Web: www.arts-crafts.com

National Association for the Self-Employed
P.O. Box 612067
DFW Airport
Dallas, TX 75261
Phone: (800) 232–6273
Web: www.nase.org

National Craft Association
1945 East Ridge Road, Suite 5178
Rochester, NY 14622
Phone: (716) 266–5472
Fax: (716) 785–3231
Phone: (800) 715–9594
Fax: (800) 318–9410
Web: www.craftassoc.com

Book Publishers

Betterway Books
F&W Publications, Inc.
1507 Dana Avenue
Cincinnati, OH 45207
Phone: (513) 531–2690
Fax: (513) 531–4082
Phone: (800) 289–0963
Web: www.fwpublications.com

IDG Books
Hungry Minds
909 Third Avenue
New York, NY 10022
Phone: (800) 762–2974
Canada: (800) 667–1115
Web: www.idgbooks.com

Interweave Press
201 East Fourth Street
Loveland, CO 80537
Phone: (303) 669–7672
Fax: (303) 667–8317
Web: www.interweave.com

Krause Publications
700 East State Street
Iola, WI 54990
Phone: (715) 445–2214
Fax: (715) 445–4087
Phone: (800) 258–0929
Web: www.krause.com

Maximum Press
605 Silverthorn Road
Gulf Breeze, FL 32561
Phone: (850) 934–0819
Fax: (850) 934–9981
Phone: (800) 989–6733
E-mail: moreinfo@maxpress.com
Web: www.maxpress.com

Nolo Press
950 Park Street
Berkeley, CA 94710
Phone: (510) 549–1976

Fax: (510) 548–5902
E-mail: info@nolo.com
Web: www.nolo.com

North Light Books
F&W Publications, Inc.
1507 Dana Avenue
Cincinnati, OH 45207
Phone: (513) 531–2690
Fax: (513) 531–4082
Phone: (800) 289–0963
Web: www.fwpublications.com

Osborne/McGraw-Hill
2600 Tenth Street
Berkeley, CA 94710
Phone: (800) 227–0900
Web: www.osborne.com

John Wiley & Sons, Inc.
605 Third Avenue
New York, NY 10158
Phone: (212) 850–6000
Phone: (800) 225–5945
E-mail: info@wiley.com
Web: www.wiley.com

Computer Companies

Ace Computers
1425 East Algonquin Road
Arlington Heights, IL 60005
Phone: (847) 952–6900
Fax: (847) 952–6901
Phone: (877) 223–2667
Web: www.acecomputers.com

Acer America Corporation
2641 Orchard Parkway
San Jose, CA 95134
Phone: (408) 432–6200
Fax: (408) 922–2933
Web: www.acer.com/us

Adamant Computers
4572 Renaissance Parkway
Cleveland, OH 44128
Phone: (216) 595–1211
Tech Support: (216) 595–9985
Fax: (216) 595–1430
Phone: (800) 236–3550
Web: www.adamant.com

American Business Services
9997 Rose Hill Road
Whittier, CA 90601
Phone: (562) 695–8823
Fax: (562) 695–8923
Phone: (800) 876–8088
Tech Support: (800) 685–3471
E-mail: sales@abspc.com
Web: www.buyabs.com

Americomp
5380 East Naiman Parkway
Solon, OH 44139
Phone: (440) 498–9620
Fax: (440) 498–9630
Phone: (800) 217–2667
Web: www.acompinc.com

Apple Computer
1 Infinite Loop
Cupertino, CA 95014
Phone: (408) 996–1010
Phone: (800) 692–7753
Web: www.apple.com

Compaq
20555 SH 249
Houston, TX 77070
Phone: (800) 888–5858
Web: www.athomecompaq.com

Compaq Factory Outlet
10251 North Freeway
Houston, TX 77037
Phone: (800) 658–1131
Fax: (713) 927–6798
Tech Support: (800) 652–6672
Web: www.compaqworks.com

CompSource
3241 Superior Avenue
Cleveland, OH 44114
Phone: (216) 566–7767
Fax: (216) 619–7117
Phone: (800) 413–7361
Web: www.c-source.com

Comp-U-Plus Direct
20 Robert Pitt Drive
Monsey, NY 10952
Phone: (914) 352–8100
Fax: (914) 352–0076
Phone: (800) 287–2323
Phone: (800) 287–8786
Web: www.compuplus.com

CompUSA, Inc.
14951 North Dallas Parkway
Dallas, TX 77269
Phone: (800) 266–7872
Web: www.compusa.com

CVT, Inc.
110 Hamel Road
P.O. Box 14
Hamel, MN 55340
Phone: (888) 770–0500
Web: www.cvtinc.com

Dell USA
1 Dell Way
Round Rock, TX 78682
Phone: (800) 999–3355
Web: www.dell.com

Enpower
18537 East Gale Avenue, #8
City of Industry, CA 91748
Phone: (626) 912–4288
Phone: (800) 997–2258
Web: www.enpower.com

Gateway 2000
610 Gateway Drive
North Sioux City, SD 57049
Phone: (605) 232–2000
Fax: (605) 232–2023
Phone: (800) 846–4208
Web: www.gateway.com

Hewlett-Packard Corporation
3000 Hanover Street
Palo Alto, CA 94034

Phone: (650) 857–1501
Fax: (650) 857–5518
Phone: (800) 752–0900
Web: www.hp.com

Hitachi PC Corporation
1565 Barber Lane
Milpitas, CA 95035
Phone: (800) 555–6820
Web: www.hitachipc.com

iDot.com
Medialand Systems, Inc.
30995 Huntwood Avenue, Suite 302
Hayward, CA 94544
Phone: (510) 475–7868
Fax: (510) 475–9116
Web: www.idot.com

IBM Personal Computer Corporation
3039 Cornwallis
Research Triangle Park, NC 27709
Phone: (888) 426–5800
Web: www.pc.ibm.com/us

InfoGOLD
1830 Houret Court
Milpitas, CA 95035
Phone: (800) 888–6615
Web: www.infogold.com

Legend Micro, Inc.
3200 South Arlington Road
Akron, OH 44319
Phone: (800) 935–9305
Web: www.legendmicro.com

Mars Technologies
705 Main Street
Hackensack, NJ 07601
Phone: (888) 627–7832
Web: www.mars-tech.com

Micron Electronics
906 East Karcher Road
Nampa, ID 83687
Phone: (208) 893–3434
Phone: (888) 224–4247
Web: www.micronpc.com

Tempest Micro
18760 East Amar Road, #188
Walnut, CA 91789
Phone: (909) 595–0550
Fax: (909) 595–5425
Phone: (800) 818–5163
Customer Service: (800) 848–5167
Web: www.tempestmicro.com

Toshiba America Information Systems
Computer Systems Division
9740 Irvine Boulevard
Irvine, CA 92618
Phone: (949) 583–3000
Phone: (800) 547–7777
Web: www.computers.toshiba.com

Craft Supplies

Craft Catalog
P.O. Box 1069
Reynoldsburg, OH 43068
Phone: (740) 964–6210
Fax: (740) 964–6212

Phone: (800) 777–1442
Fax: (800) 955–5915
E-mail: sales@craftcatalog.com
Web: www.craftcatalog.com

Earth Guild
33 Haywood Street
Asheville, NC 28801
Phone: (828) 255–7818
Fax: (828) 255–8593
Phone: (800) 327–8448
E-mail: inform@earthguild.com or
catalog@earthguild.com
Web: www.earthguild.com

Enterprise Art
P.O. Box 2918
Largo, FL 33779
Phone: (727) 536–1492
Phone: (800) 366–2218
Fax: (800) 366–6121
E-mail: custserv@enterpriseart.com
Web: www.enterpriseart.com

Factory Direct Craft Supply
315 Conover Drive
Franklin, OH 45005
Phone: (937) 743–5855
Fax: (937) 743–5500
Phone: (800) 252–5223
Fax: (800) 269–8741
Web: www.factorydirectcraft.com

Jerry's Artarama
P.O. Box 58638J
Raleigh, NC 27658
Phone: (919) 878–6782

Fax: (919) 837–9565
Phone: (800) 827–8478
Web: www.jerrysartarama.com

National Artcraft Company
7996 Darrow Road
Twinsburg, OH 44087
Phone: (330) 963–6011
Fax: (330) 963–6711
Phone: (888) 937–2723
Fax: (800) 292–4916
E-mail: nationalartcraft@worldnet.att.net
Web: www.nationalartcraft.com

Sax Arts & Crafts
2725 South Moorland Road
New Berlin, WI 53151
Phone: (800) 558–6696
Fax: (800) 328–4729
Web: www.saxarts.com

Sunshine Discount Crafts
12335 Sixty-second Street North
Largo, FL 33773
Phone: (727) 538–2878
Fax: (727) 531–2739
Phone: (800) 729–2878
E-mail: sunshinecrafts@hypernetusa.net
Web: www.sunshinecrafts.com

Direct Sales Outlets: Business and Office Equipment and Supplies

1-800-Batteries
9393 Gateway Drive
Reno, NV 89511
Phone: (775) 746–6140
Fax: (775) 746–6156
Phone: (888) 205–0093
Web: www.1800batteries.com

Abbot Office Systems
5012 Asbury Avenue
P.O. Box 688
Farmingdale, NJ 07727
Phone: (732) 938–6000
Fax: (732) 938–4419
Phone: (800) 631–2233

Fidelity Products Company
5601 International Parkway
P.O. Box 155
Minneapolis, MN 55440
Phone: (800) 328–3034
Customer Service: (800) 554–3013
Fax: (800) 842–2725

Global Industrial Equipment
1070 Northbrook Parkway
Suwanee, GA 30174
Phone: (770) 995–0007
Phone: (800) 645–1232
After-Order Service: (800) 645–2986
Fax: (800) 336–3818
E-mail: service@globalindustrial.com

Hello Direct
5893 Rue Ferrari
San Jose, CA 95138
Phone: (800) 444–3556
Fax: (800) 456–2566
E-mail: xpressit@hihello.com
(General) or
hitech@hihello.com (Tech Support)
Web: www.hello-direct.com

Nebs, Inc.
500 Main Street
Groton, MA 01471
Phone: (800) 225–6380
Customer Service: (800) 225–9540
Fax: (800) 234–4324
Web: www.nebs.com

Office Equipment Outlet
285 Industrial Drive
Wauconda, IL 60084
Phone: (800) 553–2112
Fax: (800) 541–3470
Web: www.oeo.com

Quill Corporation
(Rockies and East)
P.O. Box 4700
Lincolnshire, IL 60197
Phone: (708) 634–4800
Customer Service: (708) 634–8000
Fax: (708) 634–5708
Phone: (800) 789–1331
Customer Service: (800) 789–8965
Fax: (800) 789–8955
Web: www.quillcorp.com

Quill Corporation
(West of Rockies)
P.O. Box 50-050
Ontario, CA 91761
Phone: (714) 998–3200
Fax: (714) 634–5708
Phone: (800) 789–1331
Customer Service: (800) 789–8965
Fax: (800) 789–8955
Web: www.quillcorp.com

Viking Office Products
24 Thompson Road
East Windsor, CT 06088
Phone: (800) 711–4242
Web: www.vikingop.com

Walsh Envelope Company
478 Bethel Avenue
Aston, PA 19014
Phone: (610) 364–3150
Fax: (610) 364–3190
Phone: (800) 879–2574
Fax: (800) 925–7494
Web: www.walshenvelopes.com

Direct Sales Outlets: Computer Products

CDW Computer Centers, Inc.
200 North Milwaukee Avenue
Vernon Hills, IL 60061
Phone: (800) 830–4239
Web: www.cdw.com

Comp Direct
417 Fifth Avenue
New York, NY 10016
Phone: (212) 696–4777
Fax: (212) 696–5820
Phone: (800) 931–7070
Web: www.compdirect.com

ComputerGate International
2960 Gordon Avenue
Santa Clara, CA 95051
Phone: (408) 730–0673
Fax: (408) 730–0735
E-mail: cgate@computergate.com
Web: www.computergate.com

Computer Outlet Worldwide, Inc.
15451 Redhill Avenue, Suite C
Tustin, CA 92780
Phone: (714) 259–5959
Fax: (714) 259–5955
Phone: (877) 850–2001
Web: www.compuoutlet.com

Global Computer Supplies
2318 East Del Amo Boulevard
Compton, CA 90220
Phone: (310) 603–2266
Fax: (310) 637–6191
Phone: (800) 845–6225
Customer Service: (800) 227–1246
Web: www.globalcomputer.com

Mac Mall
2555 West 190th Street
Torrance, CA 90504
Phone: (310) 354–5600
Phone: (800) 222–2808
Web: www.macmall.com

MegaHaus
2201 Pine Drive
Dickinson, TX 77539
Phone: (281) 534–3919
Tech Support: (281) 534–2630
Fax: (281) 534–6580
Phone: (800) 786–1157
Order Inquiry: (800) 786–1192
E-mail: sales@megahaus.com
Web: www.megahaus.com

PC Mall
2555 West 190th Street
Torrance, CA 90504
Phone: (310) 354–5600
Fax: (310) 225–4004
Phone: (800) 863–3282
Web: www.pcmall.com

PC Zone
707 South Grady Way
Renton, WA 98055
Phone: (425) 430–3000
Phone: (800) 408–9663
Customer Service: (800) 248–9948
Web: www.zones.com

Q-Tech
PC/Mac Supplies Division
Quill Corporation
100 Schelter Road
Lincolnshire, IL 60069
Phone: (800) 789–1331
Customer Service: (800) 789–8965
Fax: (800) 789–8955
Web: www.quillcorp.com

TigerDirect
7795 West Flagler Street, Suite 35
Miami, FL 33144
Phone: (305) 415–2202
Fax: (305) 228–3395
Phone: (888) 335–4062
Web: www.tigerdirect.com

Magazines

American Artist
1515 Broadway
New York, NY 10036
Phone: (212) 536–5164
Subscriptions:
1 Color Court
Marion, OH 43305
(800) 745–8922

American Craft
72 Spring Street
New York, NY 10012
Phone: (212) 274–0630
Fax: (212) 274–0650
Subscriptions:
P.O. Box 3000
Denville, NJ 07834
(888) 313–5527

The Artist's Magazine
F&W Publications, Inc.
1507 Dana Avenue
Cincinnati, OH 45207
Phone: (513) 531–2690
Fax: (513) 531–2902
E-mail: tamedit@aol.com

Arts & Crafts
Krause Publications
700 East State Street
Iola, WI 54990
Phone: (715) 445–2214
Fax: (715) 445–4087
Phone: (800) 258–0929
Web: www.krause.com

Computer Buyer's Guide and Handbook
1410 Broadway, Twenty-first Floor
New York, NY 10018
Phone: (212) 807–8220
Fax: (212) 807–1098
Subscriptions:
P.O. Box 5020
Brentwood, NJ 37024
Phone: (888) 270–7652
Web: www.techworthy.com

Computer Shopper
28 East Twenty-eighth Street
New York, NY 10016
Phone: (212) 503–3900
Fax: (212) 503–3995
Web: www.cshopper.com
Subscriptions:
P.O. Box 52565
Boulder, CO 80322

Phone: (303) 604–7445
Fax: (303) 604–0518
Phone: (800) 274–6384
Fax: (850) 683–4094
E-mail: subhelp@computershopper.com
Web: www.subscribe.cshopper.com

Crafts

14901 Heritagecrest Way
Bluffdale, UT 84065
Phone: (801) 984–2070
Fax: (801) 984–2080
E-mail: editor@craftsmag.com
Web: www.craftsmag.com

Crafts 'n Things

Clapper Publishing Company, Inc.
2400 Devon, Suite 375
Des Plaines, IL 60018
Phone: (847) 635–5800
Phone: (800) 272–3871
Web: www.craftideas.com
Subscriptions:
P.O. Box 420235
Palm Coast, FL 32142
Phone: (800) 444–0441

The Crafts Report

300 Water Street
P.O. Box 1992
Wilmington, DE 19899
Phone: (302) 656–2209
Fax: (302) 656–4894
Subscriptions:
Phone: (800) 777–7098
Web: www.craftsreport.com

Decorative Artist's Workbook

F&W Publications, Inc.
1507 Dana Avenue
Cincinnati, OH 45207
Phone: (513) 531–2690
Fax: (513) 531–2902
E-mail: dawedit@fwpubs.com
Web: www.decorativeartist.com

Entrepreneur

12 West Thirty-first Street, #1100
New York, NY 10001
Phone: (212) 563–8080
Fax: (212) 563–3852
Subscriptions:
P.O. Box 50368
Boulder, CO 80322
Phone: (800) 274–6229
E-mail: subscribe@
entrepreneurmag.com

HOMEBusiness Journal

9584 Main Street
Holland Patent, NY 13354
E-mail: letters@homebusinessjournal.net
Web: www.homebusinessjournal.net
Subscriptions:
Phone: (800) 756–8484
E-mail: subscriptions@
homebusinessjournal.net

Home Business Magazine

9061 Five Harbors Drive
Huntington Beach, CA 92646
Web: www.homebusinessmag.com
Subscriptions:

P.O. Box 18449
Anaheim, CA 92817
Phone: (714) 693–1866
Fax: (714) 693–9704

Inc.

38 Commercial Wharf
Boston, MA 02210
Phone: (617) 248–8000
E-mail: editors@inc.com
Web: www.inc.com
Subscriptions:
P.O. Box 3136
Harlan, IA 51593
Phone: (515) 242–0297
Phone: (800) 234–0999
E-mail:
ICMcustserv@cdsfulfillment.com

PC Magazine

28 East Twenty-eighth Street
New York, NY 10016
Phone: (212) 503–3500
West Coast: (650) 513–8000
E-mail: pcmag@ziffdavis.com
Web: www.pcmag.com
Subscriptions:
P.O. Box 54070
Boulder, CO 80322
Phone: (303) 665–8930
Fax: (303) 604–0518
Phone: (800) 289–0429
Fax: (850) 683–4094
E-mail: subhelp@pcmag.com
Web: www.subscribe.pcmag.com

PC World

501 Second Street, #600
San Francisco, CA 94107
Phone: (415) 243–0500
Fax: (415) 442–1891
E-mail: letters@pcworld.com
Subscriptions:
P.O. Box 37571
Boone, IA 50037
Fax: (415) 882–0936
Phone: (800) 825–7595
E-mail: pcwcustserv@cdsfulfillment.com

ProCrafter

Krause Publications
700 East State Street
Iola, WI 54990
Phone: (715) 445–2214
Fax: (715) 445–4087
Phone: (800) 258–0929
Web: www.krause.com

Smart Computing

Sandhills Publishing Company
131 West Grand Drive
P.O. Box 85380
Lincoln, NE 68501
Fax: (402) 479–2104
E-mail: editor@smartcomputing.com
Web: www.smartcomputing.com
Subscriptions:
Fax: (402) 479–2193
Phone: (800) 733–3809
Web: www.smartcomputing.com

Multifunction Peripherals

Brother International Corporation
100 Somerset Corporate Boulevard
Bridgewater, NJ 08807
Phone: (908) 704–1700
Fax: (908) 575–8790
Web: www.brother.com

Canon Computer Systems, Inc.
2995 Redhill Avenue
Costa Mesa, CA 92626
Phone: (714) 438–3000
Fax: (714) 438–3099
Phone: (800) 652–2666
Web: www.usa.canon.com

Hewlett-Packard Corporation
3000 Hanover Street
Palo Alto, CA 94304
Phone: (800) 527–3753
Web: www.hp.com

Sharp Electronics Corporation
Sharp Plaza
P.O. Box 650
Mahwah, NJ 07430
Fax: (201) 529–8413
Phone: (800) 237–4277
Web: www.sharp-usa.com

Toshiba America Information Systems, Inc.
Electronic Imaging Division
P.O. Box 19724
Irvine, CA 92718
Phone: (714) 583–3000
Fax: (714) 583–3499
Phone: (800) 468–6744
Web: www.toshiba.com

Xerox
Xerox Square 05C
Rochester, NY 14644
Phone: (716) 423–5090
Fax: (716) 427–5400
Phone: (800) 822–2979
Web: www.xerox.com

U.S. Government

Federal Web Locator
Web: www.infoctr.edu/fwl

FedWorld Information Network
Web: www.fedworld.gov

GovSpot
Web: www.govspot.com

Internal Revenue Service
Forms and Publications
Phone: (800) 829–3676
Web: www.irs.ustreas.gov

Internal Revenue Service
Eastern Area Distribution Center
P.O. Box 85074
Richmond, VA 23261

Internal Revenue Service
Central Area Distribution Center
P.O. Box 8903
Bloomington, IL 61702

Internal Revenue Service
Western Distribution Center
Rancho Cordova, CA 95743

Small Business Administration
409 Third Street, Southwest
Washington, DC 20416
Phone: (800) 827–5722
Web: www.sbaonline.sba.gov

Superintendent of Documents
U.S. Government Printing Office
Washington, DC 20402
Phone: (202) 512–0132
Web: www.gpoaccess.gov

U.S. Copyright Office
Library of Congress
101 Independence Avenue,
Southeast
Washington, DC 20559
Phone: (202) 707–3000
Voice Mail: (202) 707–9100
Web: www.lcweb.loc.gov/copyright

U.S. Patent and Trademark Office
Phone: (703) 308–4357
Phone: (800) 786–9199
Web: www.uspto.gov

Index

for record keeping, 131
supplier for, 93–94
vehicle mileage log, 119

G

galleries/gift shops
    for craft displays, 197–98
    and marketing plan, 109–10
    sales to, 192–93
goal setting
    and business plan, 97, 102
    and managing business, 155–56
growth of business, 29–30
    and new product development, 206–8

H

hardware overview, computer
    diskette (floppy) drives, 140
    hard drives, 139–40
    memory, 139
    microprocessors, 138–39
    monitors, 141–42
    peripherals, 143
    printers, 142
health insurance, 87
hobby vs. business, 8
home-based business
    business vs. personal life, 36–37
    growth of, 19–20
    isolation of working alone, 22–23

pros/cons of, 20–23
technology related to, 19–20
time spent working, 20
See also craft business
home office tax treatment, 113–17
    business percentage, calculation
        of, 115
    exclusive use, 115
    limitations, 117
    principal place of business, 114
    regular use, 114
    related expenses, 116
    separate structures, 115
    trade or business use, 115
homeowner's insurance policy, 86
hourly rates, 60

I

Imation SuperDisk, 140
independent contractors, 33–35
inkjet printer, 142
insurance
    disability and health, 87
    finding agent, 87
    homeowner's policy, 86
    liability and life, 86–87
    vehicle and equipment
        coverage, 86
intellectual property, protection
    of, 87–88
interim filing system, 168–70

Internet, 203–6
invoices, for billing, 66
IRS
    listing of publications, 131
    regulations, and independent
        contractors, 33–35

L

labor, 60
laser printer, 142
leasing vehicle, tax treatment, 119
legal aspects of business, 77–94
    attorneys, 84–85
    business structures, types of, 77–80
    contracts, 93–94
    copyright, 90–92
    insurance, 85–87
    licenses and permits, 84
    naming business, 81–84
    patents, 89–90
    trademarks, 88–89
    zoning ordinances, 81
letterhead and logo design, 183–84
liability insurance, 86
libraries, public, 11–12
licenses, for operation of
    business, 6, 81–84
life insurance, 87
limited liability company, 80

M

magazine advertising, 200

mail, overnight delivery of, 19–20
mail order, for office supplies, 72
management of business, 2, 16
    business communication, 183–85
    follow-up, 185
    procrastination, 186
management of business problems,
    171–73
    avoiding complication, 172–73
    and goal setting, 7–8, 155–56
    problem identification, 172
    and productivity, 173
management plan
    describing members of business,
        106–7
    identification of limitations, 108
    list of professional/business
        associates, 107–8
    narrative of skills/experience, 107
marketing, 187–210
    advertising, 199–203
    analysis, 188–90
    craft fairs and trade shows, 191–92
    creating a reputation, 187–88
    dress for success, 192
    helpful organizations, 193–94
    hiring a sales rep, 192–93
    Internet, 203
    new product development, 206–8
    publicity, 193–94
    public relations, 195–97
    sales to shops and galleries, 190–91

selling seasons, 191

starting small and local, 189–90

Marketing on the Internet, 205

marketing plan, 108–10

determination of market
share, 109–10

identification of competition, 108

identification of markets, 108–9

markup, price, 190–91

memory, of computers, 139

Micron Electronics, 137

Micron University, 137

microprocessors, for computers,
138–39

Microsoft Office, 144

mileage log, for vehicle use, 120

monitors, computer, 141–42

multifunctional peripheral, 143

N

naming business, 81–84

mistakes in choosing names, 83–84

registration of business name,
82–83

NEBS, Inc., 94

net worth, statement of, 43–45, 102

new product development, 206–8

news releases

elements of, 195–97

form for, 196

newspaper advertising, 194, 200, 202

O

office, 26–27

computer-related supplies for, 121

supplies for, 27

tax treatment. *See* home office tax
treatment

organizational plan, of business
plan, 101–2

overhead, 59–60

overnight delivery, 19–20

ownership, and copyright, 90

P

partnership, 78–79

advantages/disadvantages of, 78–79

agreement, 79

limited liability company, 80

part-time business, advantages of, 9–10

patents, 89–90

attorneys/agents for, 90

PC Magazine, 136

PC World, 136

Pentium II, 138

Pentium III, 138

Pentium 4, 138

peripherals, computer hardware, 143

permits, for operation of business, 6, 84

personal financial statement, 43–45, 102

form for, 44

prices, competitive, 97

pricing policy, 58–63
  direct costs, 59
  equation, 62
  labor, 60
  overhead, 59–60
  profit, 60–61
  reducing costs, 63
printers, computer, 142
pro forma balance sheet, 48–49
procrastination, in business
    management, 186
production/sales/income report, 173–76
  form for, 175
productivity, 173–83
  analysis of, 173, 174, 176–83
  control of, 176–78
  improvement, 178
  production/sales/income
      report, 173–76
  ready-made components, 182–83
professionalism
  and marketing of reputation, 187–89
  vs. amateurism, 8
profit, 60–61
  and cost reduction, 63
profit-and-loss statement
  to analyze productivity, 173
  financial plan, 45–48, 102, 106
  form for, 47
property
  depreciation of, 123–26
  intellectual, protection of, 87–88

public relations, 195–97
  news releases, 195–97
publicity, 193–94
  donating work, 198
  media for, 194
  places to show work, 197–98
  volunteering, 198
purchasing, 71–75
  discounts, 71
  from local business, 71
  office supplies, 72
  time frame for, 71

Q

Quill Corporation, 72

R

radio advertising, 200
ready-made components, for craft
    production, 182–83
record keeping
  business expenses, 126–28
  cash accounting, 126
  example of bookkeeping
      system, 127–28
  income/expenses record, 129
  rules for, 126
  for taxation, 124–25
  vehicle mileage log, 118–19
renting vehicle, tax treatment, 121

About the Author

Kenn Oberrecht acquired management skills by working for six years in the corporate world, as an office manager for American Materials Corporation in Fairfield, Ohio, and as a production control supervisor for General Electric Company's Large Jet Engine Division in Evendale, Ohio. He concurrently attended the University of Cincinnati Evening College, where he earned A.A. and B.S. degrees, and later attended the University of Alaska, where he earned B.A. and M.A. degrees.

While in graduate school, Kenn began framing pictures, designing woodworking projects, and establishing his home-based business in his spare time. He and his wife, Pat, moved to the Oregon coast in 1975, where he has run a diversified full-time home-based business ever since.

His project designs, feature articles, and photographs have appeared in numerous home-and-workshop magazines, including *The American Woodworker, Black & Decker Build It!, Craftsman at Home, Decks & Backyard Projects, How To, The Homeowner, Popular Mechanics, Popular Projects, Woodworker,* and *Workbench.* He is the author of more than two dozen books and revised editions—including the *Home Book of Picture Framing,* second edition—and is a director and past president of the National Association of Home and Workshop Writers.

Help Us Keep This Guide Up to Date

Every effort has been made by the author and editors to make this guide as accurate and useful as possible. However, many things can change after a guide is published—establishments close, phone numbers change, facilities come under new management, etc.

We would love to hear from you concerning your experiences with this guide and how you feel it could be made better and be kept up to date. While we may not be able to respond to all comments and suggestions, we'll take them to heart and we'll make certain to share them with the author. Please send your comments and suggestions to the following address:

The Globe Pequot Press
Reader Response/Editorial Department
246 Goose Lane
P.O. Box 480
Guilford, CT 06437

Or you may e-mail us at:

editorial@GlobePequot.com

Thanks for your input!

TIME FOR A CHANGE?

I f you're interested in becoming your own boss, changing careers, earning extra cash, or just adding some excitement to your life, this informative series provides the tools you need to launch and maintain a successful home business. Each book is filled with insider information from professionals in the know, and includes:

- Advice on how to attract first-time customers, maintain a loyal client base, and price services competitively and profitably
- Details on start-up costs and zoning regulations
- Helpful, easy-to-use worksheets and questionnaires
- Listings of trade contacts and organizations

"I highly recommend reading [this] series. . . . All of these works delve into marketing, financial management, and just about anything you would need to know to take the plunge in a new venture."

—Steve Rubel, *Mac Home Journal*

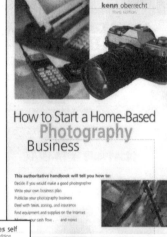

Titles in this series:

For more information or to order, visit your local bookstore or contact:

Telephone: 800–243–0495 • www.GlobePequot.com